Revelations of the Lord to his Most High Priest for his Disciples in Truth

ISBN-13 ; 978-1-466288478
ISBN-10 ; 1466288477

3

In Memorandum

In Memory of the many of the faithful disciples who were martyred in Theban faith the first three hundred years after Yeshua (Jesus) was crucified. There are many who do not know the actual truths, disciples of Jesus **COULD NOT** tell, for they were executed by an Empire bent on conquering and instituting it's authority over their cultures and their faiths. Though some have proclaimed this name of Theban unto themselves, some of the Gods, angels and the Goddess Isis within their religion are not of real Lord in heaven, or any of the Roman and Greek mythological invented hypocrisies. There is but one **LORD** and one **FAITH** given by the Father in heaven unto mankind and his name is Amen-Ra, as told to the Pharaoh Ahmose I in the 16th century b.c. Atum-Ra, was his name in the Old Kingdom dynasties, and is, as written upon the Pyramid Texts at Giza. Thebanism has nothing to do with any pagan religion, wicca, or satanism as many presume, for this faith though it had it's own evolution, much as all other belief systems have had, was one that taught that we are Gods, each responsible for our own destiny, on earth, and the afterlife. Many cults have used the names of the holy and shown their ignorance in what they call the words of the holy but clearly show many psychological blasphemies within them. "Blasphemies," because they give the holy of heaven a nature which is so degrading that this evaluation in their books could have only come from the devil or man itself. This book, is dedicated to all the Theban faith martyrs who died on September 22, 286 a.d., at the hands of the Roman Empire. The **THEBAN LEGION** consisted of 6,600 "saints," Egyptian disciples of Jesus, lead by Captain Maurice who in history has mistakenly been referred to as the leader of "Theban Christians." The huge majority of these disciples were of Egyptian descent, soldiers in the Roman Army stationed at Thebes, Egypt. **DISCIPLES,** not "servants" of Jesus, which became the doctrines of Roman Christianity less than 50 years later. As disciples, they were free men of the Lord, living in the doctrines of the Son of Amen-Ra. Yezua. (Yeshua / Jesus)

The blood of ALL the innocent killed over the course of "20" centuries by self-righteous religions cry out for **JUSTICE, TRUTH** and **REVELATIONS**. Since 1823, we now know the "truths" which lay buried and upon monuments that could not be read in hieroglyphics, the written language of ancient Egypt, but in this year, it's language was deciphered. "There," discoveries revealed the ancient faith in the holy Father in heaven, and also revealed who Jesus "actually" had been.

It has come time to "resurrect" the **HOLY FAITH** of the **FATHER IN HEAVEN** just as it was in the **BEGINNING**..

*Note;

The Theban Legion had "3" commanders. Mauritius (Maurice), Candidus, and Exupernis. Maurice being Captain of the Legion. Emperor Maximian was head of the Roman Empire in 286 a.d. Though this page is to the memory of the Theban Legionaries who gave up their lives rather than kill the innocent, let us not forget the MILLIONS who were " also " disciples of Yeshua that the Roman Empire and it's soldiers, and later "church," chose to slaughter simply because it saw them as a threat to their rule throughout the regions they had conquered. Of these sects of faithful disciples of Yeshua were the Copts, Arians, Gnostics, Yeshuans, Yezuites, Cathars, Jewish converts, Egyptian Therapuet Monks, Essenes, **"TRUE"** Greek Christians, and Catholics (not Roman) of the Church of Edessa and many , many , more throughout the world that the slaughters are so numerous to mention. To them and their **SACRIFICE,** devotion in faith and lost of life, will "now" be known to the world who will know the truths of the Kingdom of the Lord in heaven they lost their lives on earth to preserve.

Rest in Peace

Table of Contents

Comments by Author on the Chapters written in Index @ Chapter's end

Sacred Truths of the Monk Yeshua

(Jesus)

SACRED WORDS
OF THE
LORD OF CREATION,
AMEN-RA

**FOR THE DISCIPLES OF AMEN IN YEZUA
(YESHUA)**

Neologism of Thoth

1 In the beginning, was a deep void, and nothing filled the vastness of this abyss but, "darkness."

2 A darkness, pitch black, and without light that later would be called Nun.

3 And the void gave way to the forces of light, a bright and shining power which made itself to overcome darkness.

4 Born of itself, a Spirit was it's being, invisible, except when it shone upon the vast darkness. When the light saw it was by itself, it coughed and created two other lights, and called one of them Shu, and the other, Tefnut.

5 And he said unto them, "You will be my Gods, my angels, and holy spirits upon all I create, and all that you do on my behalf."

6 And the Creator called their shadows upon the darkness "day," and the darkness, "night."

7 To assure that the light would never succumb to darkness, the creator made a Sun, in the midst of the darkness.

8 "This voiced the creator, will be RA, that which is of me but not invisible that the darkness will never reign over all things again.

9 I am the Atum and the Amen, the Alpha and Omega, the beginning and the end.

10 The Lord of Creation unto all things for I am the I am.

11 In the sun, all that I create will remember who I am, for I will call myself the same as I have called it with the authority of my command.

12 So be it in the purity of rays of sunlight for I am the Lord, Amen-Ra."

13 Being of spirit, it gave charge to Shu and Tefnut to help fill the empty darkness with the beauty of heavenly bodies.

14 Planets, stars, galaxies began to fill the void and the suns began to make much grow upon them of trees, grasses, and waters.

15 Ra coughed upon them to fill them with all manner of living things, on land and in the waters, of every form after some planets formed and cooled.

16 Ra saw all he had created and his angels had helped him with and said it was

good, for now the vast nothingness gave way to the movement of life and light.

17 Such beauty did Ra create that upon one of these planets it's spirit wanted to dwell. A place Ra called "Earth."

18 Here Ra told his Gods, is OUR paradise, and I will make you bodies that you may be born to enjoy all I have made. As spirit I will dwell amongst you.

19 You Shu, will I make into a male, for from you will come the seed to create just as I, and Tefnut will I make a woman, for from her womb will her seed unite with your own to make that which is part of you both.

20 For I have seen the planets, the stars, and all I have created and from two they mold into one in beauty, and you will grow up on a world of my creation.

21 You both are of the spirit I will make into the flesh to create a link to all I create, a being of both realities, spirit and flesh will I make you.

22 In time, Shu and Tefnut bore a child to the world. A daughter they called Nut.

23 The Goddess, grew up and came time that she was want for a man. The Lord seeing that Nut needed her own companion, created Geb of the ground, as he could not bear him into the flesh as a grown man.

24 A man, of the ground to be in the flesh and was not of the spirit.

25 As time passed, the union of Geb and Nut produced five children, the lives of the Gods, Osiris, Seth, Horus and Goddesses, Isis, and Nephthys.

26 When the children of Geb and Nut became adults, Osiris took Isis as his wife, just as Seth took Nephthys to be his. Pure in the flesh and spirit.

27 Horus never took a wife, and Ra never created one for him.

28 In time, Isis gave birth to Horus, a son, and Nephthys gave birth to Anubis, also a son.

29 Because all the children of Ra were in need of nourishment for their bodies, Ra filled the Oceans with all manner of creatures and fish.

30 On the lands, he created all manner of animals, fruit trees and plants, that which would be food for his own.

31 Here, he gave charge over the sky, land, waters, animals, ocean creatures, to those of his creation and appointed Osiris King, or Pharaoh over them on earth.

32 Time passed and Ra saw all was good and wanted to return to filling the vastness of space that was still filled with darkness.

33 Ra found out by his children that existence in the body was not like existence in the spirit and he would have to return to look after those on earth.

34 Flesh ages, is subject to the elements of the world and withered away and Ra noticed that life in the flesh was harsh, even ceasing to exist in body.

35 He called this transition back into the spirit form, "death," as the flesh died but the spirit would not.

36 So he knew if he left he had to return before those on earth "died."

37 One day while creating Ra became aware of something which he had not experienced. An emotion and the cries of Osiris. Then appeared Osiris unto him in spirit.

38 Returning to earth, he questioned Seth, about where his brother Osiris was.

39 Seth replied, 'Am I my brother's keeper? How do I know."

40 The Lord said, "I have heard your brother's cries and smell his blood upon the ground and has returned to me and know it is you who has killed him.

41 For this grave injustice, will you punish yourself for what you have done for I am not the Lord of destruction, but the Lord of Creation.

42 You my son, have chosen your destiny and the outcome of your eternal existence.

43 Because you have made this ground unholy, you will dwell upon it for all eternity, only to come out in the darkness for your spirit is dark and you are blind to all I have given you. In the death of your flesh, your spirit will never leave this place.

44 Your brother Osiris will always be with me, and will not return for he has chosen to do my will in heaven, where I will set up my kingdom."

45 Millennia passed, then all the Gods and Geb upon earth went up into heaven where Ra gave of his spirit unto Geb. All returned, and when Seth died in the flesh was tossed out of heaven upon the earth for he had condemned himself.

46 Ra being the loving, and compassionate Father in heaven could not accept Seth

into his kingdom, even in forgiveness, for that which is sacred is life itself.

47 Seth had chosen his actions, despite the fact Osiris is spirit, not just flesh, and Ra for the love of his own can not blemish his kingdom with one so evil.

48 Life, is sacred. ALL life. The Lord is just to reject those who do not respect it in themselves or others.

49 A long time passed before the Lord came down to earth again, and when he did, he could not comprehend all Seth had done.

50 Creatures unlike anything he'd ever seen and Seth created beings from an animal he had put upon it.

51 Creatures of a nature much like their creator and Seth took advantage of them by subjecting them even to his realm in spirit.

52 It was clear to Ra, why Seth created such a creature. It was his way of existing outside the spirit realm by possessing these creatures.

53 Even his devils in his realm, possessed so they could escape their punishment.

54 As the Lord saw this, he could tolerate it no longer and went amongst that which Seth created in his teacher, Thoth.

55 Now Thoth was one who came from another world of Ra's creation and wise.

56 As a God upon the earth, he spread the Lord's sacred words and taught those of the Nile Valley to read and write in the sacred language of hieroglyphics.

57 He also taught them that this world was not the end to all things and each one of them could earn life in the afterlife for all eternity in the spirit.

58 While on earth, Ra chose a King, Pharaoh to be God on earth. One who was of his spirit, to reign over the peoples of Egypt.

59 Thoth, went amongst others peoples in the world to teach them the Lord's wisdoms. Many accepted them, while others, followed Seth to create religion of prejudices.

60 Because Seth nor his demons could not possess just anyone on earth who chose to live their lives in the will of the Lord in heaven.

61 To those who listened, Ra said, "Respect all life, and I will reserve a place in heaven for you.

62 Treat others as you want to be treated. For greater am I who can be 'in' you than he that is in the world.

63 I am the Lord of Creation of all things, including this fallen one called, Seth.

64 I am, that I am, the beginning and the end to all creation, good or bad. I am the Amen, you shall call RA, for I am the light of all life, spirit and flesh."

Note

Seth, or name for the "evil one," has had various spellings. In some of the ancient Egyptian sacred words he is also known as SET , or SETEKH. This version is condensed, revised and shortened from original papyri and may not contain all the holy ones within them, as the main depiction has been given as to creation and that of the teachings sent by one of the holy Gods of the Lord's creation around 6000 years ago. Thoth is a God of the Lord in heaven whom he sent unto the peoples of the Nile Valley in the era of pre-dynastic Egypt to teach his wisdom, two of which were to read and write in hieroglyphics. Because his teachings and Jesus are so oddly associated with Egyptian sacred words, he may have been " Thoth. " It is a well known fact that peoples of the Nile Valley circa 6000 to 7000 years ago were taught of eternal life and evidence of this was found in what the Egyptologist Petrie labeled the "Gerzean" era of history in the Nile Valley. It is for sure that Pharaohs wore royal robes with the sign of the " ankh " that symbolized "life" and was used thousands of years before Christians used it to symbolize the crucifixion of Jesus on the cross.

Speculation by the skeptics is that the Jesus story is nothing more than an expandsion of the story of Horus, Son of Osiris and Isis. One problem arises from this specuatory premise though, and that is "why" were so many books written by so many different authors about Jesus having been on earth? Another would be that the prophesy of Nu wouldn't mean a thing and the fact the Pharaohs wore the ankh on their robes would not have told that one day this divine child would be born. Question here arises whether the Pharaohs were not told early on that the Son of the Lord on earth would be put to death to "prove" life after death and the symbol of the ankh was not only to symbolize "life" but "how" this divine child would be put to death while on earth, and arising from it to prove the resurrection "exists."

PROPHESY

Excerpt from the ancient sacred language of hieroglyphics, a "prophesy," given by the Lord of Creation to his most holy Priest Nu, one of his chosen. Compiled and written within the Book of Ani, an Egyptian priest of the 18th dynasty around 1240 b.c. The "prophesy" of Nu, and this child to be born of the Father in heaven.

Hail, thou who makest sweet the time of the Two Lands! (Upper and Lower Egypt) Hail, dweller among the celestial food.

Hail, dweller among the beings of blue (lapis-lazuli), watch ye to protect him that is in his nest, the CHILD WHO COMETH FORTH FOR/FROM YOU. I am the jackal of jackals. I am the God, Shu.

I draw air from the presence of the Light god, from the uttermost limits of heaven, from the uttermost limits of earth, from the uttermost limits of the pinion of Nebeh bird.

May air be given unto this young DIVINE BABE. My mouth is open, I see with my eyes.

Hail, Father. Grant thou unto me the sweet breath which dwelleth in thy nostrils. I am he who embraceth that great throne which is in the city of Unu.(Hermopolis) I keep watch over the Egg of Kenken-ur (or Great Cackler name used many times in the Old Kingdom referring to the Lord of Creation). I grow and flourish as it groweth and flourisheth. I live as it liveth. I snuff the air as it snuffeth the air.   (Papyri of Nu, Sheet 12, British Museum)

Age of this prophesy? Approximately, 4500 years old. The Hebrew prophets were not ignorant of this Egyptian prophesy and "knew" that a child, Son of the Lord of Creation, (Atum-Ra>Old Kingdom dynasties, Amen-Ra > New Kingdom dynasties), would one day be born. When the Pharaoh Amenhotep IV, or "Akhenaton" abolished the old faith in Amen, (Amon) for his " Aton, " the Hyksos Ahmose I had taken as slaves in the 16th century b.c., in the 14th century b.c. called themselves "Hebrews," and were of the faithful of Amen-Ra. It is Akhenaton, Moses dealt with, written in the holy books of the Hebrews for the Lord gave him authority over Pharaoh. In later times, an uprising occurred amongst the Israelites and "faith." The Prophet Samuel, listened to "his" Lord and appointed his own "King" over the peoples. It is where

13

many truths became obscure and "lost." As Jesus said, "Not as in the BEGINNING."

IN THE PAPYRUS OF NU, SHEET 14,

Thy son Horus hath ascended thy throne and all life is with him. Millions of years minister unto him, and millions of years hold him in fear. The Company of the Gods are his servants, and they fold him in fear. The god Tem, the Governor, (Tem is Amen), the only One among the gods, hath spoken, and his word passeth not away. Horus is both the divine food and the sacrifice. He made haste to gather together the members of his father. Horus is his deliverer. Horus hath sprung from the essence of his divine Father.

WITHIN THE KING JAMES BIBLE IS WRITTEN THIS OF JESUS , (YESHUA)

Luke 1:30-31 ;

"And the angel said unto her, Fear not, Mary, for thou hast found favour with Amen. And behold, thou shalt conceive in thy womb, and bring forth a son, and shalt call his name JESUS."

Matthew 24:35 ;

"Heaven and earth shall pass away but my words shall not pass away."

Matthew 24:31 ;

"And he shall send his angels with a great sound of a trumpet, and they shall gather together his elect from the four winds, from one end of heaven to the other."

Matthew 25:31 ;

"When the Son of man shall come in his glory, and all the holy angels with him, then shall he sit upon the throne of his glory."

14

One of the overwhelming realities of religions "is," that of the many of them that exist today, will be called myths tomorrow. Religion, though, is a conception of man, FOR man. Faith is of the Lord, and "OF" the Lord. There is but one Lord. The one of heaven, and his angels, or "Gods," One of those Gods chose to go against the Lord and declared himself the Lord of earth, with his angels, or "Demons." These angels, do his will. The Hyksos, whose descendants called themselves the Hebrews, must have learned the ways of Amen-Ra in captivity, and the Pharaoh Akhenaton challenged their devotion. Though many will deny these truths, the conflict lays not in truth, but "vanity." Men have always chosen the ways of self-righteousness. To live in a delusion they own the holy ones in heaven, but they will always remain the property of all who are their faithful and not the property of mankind's vain religions. It WAS, the Hebrew peoples in ancient times that saved the doctrines of ancient Egypt for about two centuries until the Prophet Samuel, under what he stated was told to him by his Lord, appointed "David" as King over the Israelites to that of Saul. If anyone studies these words in the Torah, you will also see the "God" Samuel mislead the Hebrew peoples to believe in, as being the one in heaven, when in "fact" he was not. Moses, as did many of the hebrew peoples, accepted Amen to be the Lord in heaven, and is "why" he was on mount with Jesus when he was transfigured. We are all made in the image of God, and the words hold true, for Seth (Satan) is nothing more than a God under the Lord in heaven. He is, though, not the Creator of everything. He "is," the creator of this species called homo sapien upon this planet and he did it out of NEED to escape his punishment and out of "vanity." If you read closely the words of the ancient Hebrews, you will find this word HOST. It is used so often in script that a search of it drives a computer crazy with how many times it is mentioned. The "devil," not the Lord in heaven, created MANKIND as HIS tool he could possess as well as those of his kind, to use their "bodies." The New Testament in the bibles of the Christian religion writes of those who were "demon possessed" and Jesus (Yezua) cast them out. In Thebes, Memphis and Hermopolis, Egypt where the faith was strong in Amen-Ra, it was a practice each morning to get up and deal with the Apophis, (serpent) which desired to kill Ra, as he rose from the east each day.

15

Of course, we now know this ritual was superstition based in fear that the Sun would not rise " someday, " but we also now know where this superstition came about. Around 5 to 6 thousand b.c., a volcanic eruption was so great in the region that it must have been years before peoples of that region got to see the sun. Not every faith is without some superstitions or beliefs based in phobias. This ritual by the priests, blamed the forces of evil for this mishap they dealt with at one time and it is understandable, if " we " had been there ourselves. There have been various catastrophic events in history that in religions get blamed on some entity, because at the time they were not aware of the "physics" involved. The best EXAMPLE of TRUTH, is that which is not such a "mystery," or taboo, and like the Pyramids of Giza, should stand out to the world, as "we" should in faith. It written Jesus said we should not "hide" that faith, but be as a candle on a hill for all to see.

Jesus did some very REVEALING things while on earth to LEAD people to who he WAS, and the faith he taught. Here are a few of them for you to ponder;

1. > Called the Creator, "FATHER." Not a Jewish term, but an EGYPTIAN one. This term Father, was used for centuries by the Pharaohs and faithful of Amen-Ra.

2. > Baptism. The Egyptian priests cleansed themselves each and every morning before their prayers, for we came "out" of water in the beginning.

3. > Prayed in secret. Pharaohs "prohibited" the public from the temple(s) where each day he would commune in prayer to the Lord of Creation, "secretly."

4. > Beattitudes. Taught by many Pharaohs to the peoples that "destiny" lay in how we " behaved " and the ways we " treated " others. It was commonly known that for many centuries, Egyptians invited foreigners to Egypt, much as tourism is today.

5. > Gave us the LORD'S PRAYER, and "ended" it with the name of the "Father in heaven," AMEN. (New Kingdom Dynasties - "Amen-Ra")

6. > Resurrected people while on earth. An "act" historically on record as ONLY

having been done by the Goddess Isis protector of the children and Goddess of the "Resurrection."

7. > Taught of his death at the hands of men and the RESURRECTION. Written of in the holy books of Egypt as having happened to the god "Osiris."

8. > Called himself the Son of Amen in heaven. A "reference" MANY Pharaohs called themselves.

9. > Chose 12 Apostles. In the faith of Amen, "12 Gods" were the "council" in the Kingdom of heaven to " confer " with regarding any matter which was brought before them by the Pharaoh, including birth of a successor. "And Jesus gave them power over heaven and earth. Whatsoever they loosen on earth would be loosened in heaven whatsoever they bound on earth would be bound in heaven."

10. > Said he was not of this world. Pharaohs were said to have been "Sons of Amen in heaven" BORN of the seed of Amen (Amon), as such "not of this WORLD."

11. > Believed in the laying down of his life as a sacrifice for the peoples. Also a belief of the Pharaohs of Egypt. A few SACRIFICED themselves by death for their peoples in the hopes their sacrifice would bring prosperity.

12. > At the Last Supper he stated an Osirian rite of passage. The flesh and blood sacrifice. Bread to represent the flesh and wine to represent the blood which was done by the Pharaohs unto Osiris for having given his life to assure that others may gain entry into the afterlife and eternal life.

13. > Taught of eternal life. Egyptian belief, not taught by Jews, thousands of years old. Jesus taught, "In my Father's house are many mansions," which links him directly to the writings of the Egyptian scribe "Nebseni" within the Priest Ani of the 13th century b.c. "Book of the Dead."

14. > Belief in the " ANKH. " Symbol, worn by the Pharaohs upon their royal dress to remind them of life after death. (looks like Christian crosses worn today)

15. > Rejected being called Son of David. Was not "direct" link to King David,

17

not even through Mary, his mother, a descendant of Nazarene "gentiles."

16. > Followed Essene teachings (Some who were Egyptian Therapuet Monks). Unknown for centuries, Essenes lived at Qumran around the Dead Sea and found were many of their doctrines, many of which were "exactly" as taught by Jesus.

17. > Taught about humility. As did Egyptian priests and Pharaohs , much of which was the downfall of the Egyptian civilization. Being too kind to "outsiders."

18. > Crucified on a cross. As Pharaohs and Egyptians used the Ankh as a symbol to remind them of life after death, the cross has replaced that symbol and has the same value as that peoples of Egypt held for the ankh for thousands of years.

19. >

* REVELATION *

The Latin Vulgate, the " first " translation of Hebrew and Greek manuscripts into Latin by Jerome all contained the name of the Lord in heaven in Hebrew perspective, as "given" by the Apostles. **Amen dico** , in English is "Amen says," is written throughout the Latin Vulgate many times, when Jesus spoke and taught to the peoples in his time on earth. The PHRASE, " **VERILY I SAY UNTO YOU**" which is/was used and written by Egyptian priests thousands of years BEFORE the time of Christ is written deceptively over the Lord's name in Catholicism, has remained this way in translations of later periods. Jewish converts, of which the Apostles "were," just as Constantine and the Bishops of the Roman Catholic Church, were not AWARE that 1500 years EARLIER, a FAITH, existed in Egypt where "Amen" was the Lord of Creation, mainly, because nobody knew how to READ the ancient language of hieroglyphics.

The first translator of Hebrew and Greek manuscripts into English, William Tyndale evidently ran across this " mistake, " for on October, 1536 he was burned at stake upon the orders of the leadership of the Roman Catholic Church.

An "odd" occurrence happened in the year 1823 when the Rosetta Stone " unlocked" the language of the ancient Egyptian ivilization. Pope Leo XII cut all ties

18

with France. (translator of the Rosetta Stone was French) He also went after persecuting the Jews, having some executed. "Coincidence?" I don't think so.

Problem with " lies, " is that once "Empires" are built upon their foundation, alot of money is at stake to bring out the truth and retract them. Jesus said it another way.

"One day the rains came upon the house built on sand and it FELL."

Note

This Book of Faith is written with as much historical accuracy as possible, but because so much of Egyptian artifacts and history still remains undiscovered and that which is included, is "that" which has been uncovered and revealed to the world.

This book will shock many and will offend organized religion and their following , but TRUTH has remained in the mire long enough. Jesus taught "spirituality" and that which was taught in Egypt for close to 3000 years. A "universal" faith, and one which is not full of rules as religions are. Life is to be "enjoyed," and the one of the hardest facts for many amongst mankind is "accepting" all the Lord in heaven has done for us already. Like the devil, many live in vanity, and personally can not stand living a life without seeking attention unto themselves. That in itself, is why we in this world are subject to so many " different " religions. From the very beginning, this faith that was taught in Egypt was plain and simple. Too plain and simple for the vain persons who could not stand giving a God, (s), attention but sought an existence using fear, violence and murder to subjugate the masses. It is NOT the ways of the Lord for each person is a God unto his/herself and has been provided the tools by the Lord to make a comfortable existence unto themselves. For "that," we love him, giving praise for all he has given, and give respect for he gave it to us.

Sacred Truths of the Monk Yezua

(Yeshua in Hebrew, Yezua in Arabic)
according to his Apostles and Disciples both Jewish, Egyptian and of the World

CHAPTER 1

1 **The Book of Yezua** ,

who is called Jesus, Jesus Christ, Jesus the Christ, Savior, Yezua, Son of God, Yahweh, Prophet, Messiah, Son of Man or Yeshua in this Book relating to his life and ministry, as written by Levi, Son of Alphaeus called Matthew by Jesus along with words from his other Apostles and Disciples.

2 Within this book, is historical data, written by Amen John I, a disciple, from accounts of the Apostles, Yeshuans, Yezuites, Cathers, Copts, Essenes, Arians, Gnostics, Thebans and disciples not of Jewish lineage.

3 In the papyri of ancient Egypt, lay writings of the Osiris Nu, priest to the God on Earth, Pharaoh to the peoples of Egypt, prophesying of the coming of a divine child, a "babe" from the loins of the Father in heaven. Son, of Ra.

4 Prophesy, from the giver of life, older than the Great Pyramid itself, and of a child , who would live, breathe and dwell on earth amongst mankind,

5 Thoth a God, angel, sent of the Father in heaven upon the Nile Valley, taught this to inhabitants who lived there in the sacred language of the holy for there was no understanding of any word, for the Lord, is the WORD,

6 As he taught the sacred language of Amen, so the peoples learned to read and write upon papyri and upon stone that future generations may read of their peoples history and sacred faith.

7 So the scribes wrote of the angel who came unto the priest Nu and gave him the prophesy of the divine child. A "King" amongst all Kings and Son of Amen on earth.

8 In remembrance, he who is the chosen Pharaoh was to wear the ankh on royal robes, to remember eternal life and the prophesy of what is to come, unto all peoples.

9 Now Mary, a descendant of the royal house of Pharaohs, lived in the land of Galilee, in Nazareth of the Gentiles, of ancient lands of Egypt and Palestine south of the once great Hittite Empire, not of those mentioned by the Hebrews.

10 Of Mary's royal lineage are they who were once the Lord's Gods on earth. Line of Pharaohs before the conquest of Egypt by Persians in 341 b.c., and native kings are, Nectanebo II, Zeher, Nectanebo I, Amyrteus, Bocchoris, Pasebkhanu II, Si-Amon, Amenemypt, Paseb-khanu I, Smendes, Rameses III to XI,

11 Of the Old Kingdom, Middle, up to the New Kingdom Pharaohs, the royal house were;

12 Narmer-Menes, Aha, Zer, Zet, Udy-mu, Merpaba, Semerkhet, Qa, Hotep-ahaui, Ra-neb, Neteri-mu, Perabsen, Kha-sekhem, Ka-ra, and Kha-sekh-emwy,

13 Sa-nekht, Djoser-Neterkhet, Snefru, Shaaru, Khufu, Khafre, Men-kau-Re, Dade-f-Re, Shepses-kaf, Sebek-ka-Re, Userkaf, Sahu-Re, Shepses-ka-Re, Neferf-Re,

14 Ni-user-Re, Men-kau-Hor, Wenis, Dad-ka-Re, Ysesi Dad-ka-Re, Tety, User-ka-Re, Pepi I, Meren-Re, Pepi II, Mehti-em-saf, Neter-ka-Re, Queen Neith-aqe-rt, and hundreds un-named in the middle kingdom left to the dust of the earth.

15 Yntef I, Yntef II, Mentu-hotep I, Mentu-hotep II, Mentu-hotep III, and Mentu-hotep IV, Amonemhat I, Senusert I, Amonemhat I, Senusert II, Senusert III, Amonenhat III, Amonemha IV, and Queen Sebck-nefiu.

16 Seqemen I, Seqemen II, Seqemen III, Kames, Ahmose I, Amenhotep I, Thutmose I, Thutmose II, Queen Hatshepsut, Thutmose II, aka (Men-Kheper-RE), Amen-hotep II, Thutmose IV, Amenhotep III, Amenhotep IV, aka (Akhenaton),

17 Smenkh-Ka-Re, Tutankhamon, aka (King Tut), Ay, Haremheb, Rameses I, Seti I, aka (Setekhy I), Rameses II, Mer-ne-Ptah, Seti II, aka (Setekhy II,) Amen-mose, Si-Ptah, and Seti-nekht (Setekh-nekht), of which the like are the chosen of Amen as the Gods on earth to lead the peoples of Egypt.

18 Many more of royal blood escape this writing, as time and robbers have destroy-ed their tombs, all of the royal lineage of Mary.

19 Now Jesus, was a stepson of Joseph, who was said to be a descendant of the Hebrew King David that ruled Judea of Israel. (*Note* in Index)

20 Joseph was the son of Jacob, betroth to a woman called Mary, who was a cousin of the high Jewish priest Zacharias, by being married to Elizabeth. Joseph became the husband of Mary, before the birth of Jesus.

21 The man whom Greek faithful would later remember was he foretold by the Egyptian priest Nu. When Mary, was betrothed to Joseph,

22 An angel of the Lord told Mary she was to give birth to the child of the Holy Spirit in heaven, a child of divine prominence, having come unto her one day.

23 Mary, a just woman of devout faith, quietly accepted that which the Lord had bestowed upon her but, Joseph at first, was reluctant to ccept that Mary was with child, and being a just man, did not want Mary to become a public spectacle, or be stoned as an embarrassment, so he thought about hiding her away privately.

24 That night while he was contemplating these actions, he laid down to sleep, and as he lay asleep, an angel of Lord appeared to him in a dream saying, "Joseph, don't be afraid to take Mary to be your wife for the child which is conceived in her womb is the child of the Father in heaven.

25 She will give birth to a son, and you should give him the name of Jesus, for he will offer humanity salvation from the evils of this world and all their unholy behaviors."

26 Joseph woke up from his sleep, got up and did as the angel in the dream asked him to do and married Mary.

27 Throughout Mary's pregnancy, Joseph took care of Mary, being her husband, but refrained from any physical contact with her until she gave birth to the first born Son of the Lord, whom they named, Yeshua. (Jesus)

28 Jesus was born at the time when a brilliant, bright, and shining star in the sky shone in the eastern hemisphere. This happened "twice." Once at the time of his birth, and the other three years later, and signified the "coming out of Egypt" prophesy.

29 Egypt under the hands of conquerors at the time of Jesus' birth, made it possible for the Lord to come amongst the descendants of those who once saved his teachings from a heretic Pharaoh, though they themselves changed many of them.

Note Verse 19

In Christianity, confusion arises within the Gospels, as written, for they not only call Jesus the Son of God, but also the Son of " David " writing alot of genealogy stating a genetic connection to the Hebrew King David of Judah. Jesus "consistantly" denied it many times. " Accepting, " what Christians have proclaimed the last 20 centuries about Jesus, " BLASPHEMES, " who he truly " WAS. " He was NOT a genealogical Son of his "stepfather" who was Joseph, but of the " seed " of the most holy Father in heaven, thus NOT in any way connected to the Jewish " ancestry. " The Lord in heaven is not an entity of "labels" or one who is owned by one "culture," nor is his concern over our petty squabbles over genetic links to him for the flesh is "unimportant." It is our SPIRIT and our BEHAVIORS that concern him.

Note Verse 28

(Occurances were in 7 b.c., and 4 b.c. Another slight occurance in the heavens happened in 2 a.d.)

CHAPTER 2

1 Foretold 800 years prior to his birth by a man called Micah "where" Jesus was to be born in Bethlehem, this land was called Zebulon, but Zebulon and Bethlehem of old did not exist any longer, for Zebulon was now called Galilee and near old Bethlehem made way to a town now called, Nazareth.　(*Note* in Index)

2 One day Joseph and Mary were to go to Jerusalem to pay their taxes, as they left, shortly thereafter Mary went into labor right at the spot where Bethlehem of old stood where now an inn stood.

3 Joseph went in and asked for a room, but there were no rooms available, but the innkeeper offered a place behind the inn. On a cold night in a manger, Jesus was born. Joseph wrapped the baby in clothes to keep him warm, as this was in the middle of winter.

4 Behold, there came three wise men to Jerusalem in the days of Herod the king of Israel, "Where is he that is born King of the Jews?, for we have seen his star in the east, and have come to worship him."　(*Note* in Index)

5 When Herod the king heard these men and of their inquiry, he was troubled, as were many who were feeling the same throughout Jerusalem. Herod quickly convened together all the chief priests and scribes of the Jewish peoples and demanded they tell him where this "King" was to be born.

6 They said unto him, "It is written by a man 800 years ago named Micah, "And thou Bethlehem, in the land of Zebulon art not the least among the princes of Israel, for out of thee shall come a Governor, that shall rule my people."

7 Then the priests informed Herod that Bethlehem of Zebulon which existed 800 years before in the time of Micah did not exist anymore. Nazareth, was now close to where it existed and now there was Bethlehem in Judea. So Herod, called in the wise men to speak to them in private, diligently asking them what time the star appeared.

8 He sent them to Bethlehem of Judea and said, "Go and search diligently for the young child, and when you have found him, come and tell me where he is so that

I may come and worship him too."

9 When they had heard the king, they departed, and, lo, the star, which they saw in the northeast, guided them and came and stood over where the young child was in Galilee.   (*Note* in Index)

10 When they saw the star, they rejoiced with exceeding great joy.

11 When they entered the manger, they saw the young child with his mother, Mary, and immediately fell down to worship him, and then they opencd up their treasures and presented to him gifts of gold, frankincense, and myrrh.

12 Being warned by the Lord in heaven, Amen-Ra in a dream that they should not return to Herod, they departed into their own country another way.

13 After the wise men left, behold, an angel of the Lord appeared to Joseph in a dream while he slept, saying, "Arise, and take the young child and his mother, and flee into Egypt, and stay there until I advise you differently, for Herod will seek the young child to destroy him.

14 When he arose, he took the young child and his mother by night, and departed into Egypt,

15 And was there until the death of Herod, in 4 b.c., fulfilling that which was written by Micah, saying, "Out of Egypt have I called my son."

16 Then Herod, realized he had been mocked by the wise men. Exceeding angry, he ordered the slaying of all the children of Bethlehem, and in all the coasts thereof, from the age of two years old and under, assuming the age of this child according to the time when the wise men appeared in his presence.

17 A prophesy made by Jeremiah, a Hebrew Prophet, in a book stating,

18 "In Rama, was there a voice heard, lamentation, weeping, and great mourning of Rachel weeping for her children, and would not be comforted, because they are not."

19 When Herod died, behold, an angel of the Lord appeared again to Joseph while in Egypt in a dream,

20 Saying, "Arise, and take the young child and his mother, and go into the land of Israel, for they are dead which sought the young child's life.

21 And he arose, and took the young child and his mother, and came into the land of Israel.

22 When Joseph heard that Archelaus did reign in Judea in the room of his father Herod, he was afraid to go through there, notwithstanding, being warned by Amen in a dream, he turned aside into the parts of Galilee,

23 And came and they lived in Nazareth.

INDEX*CHAPTER 2

Note Verse 1

The "prophesics" written throughout the gospels of the Christian faith pertaining to Jesus, and "said" to have been written by the Apostles or the disciples Luke and Mark show obvious signs that the Jewish converts whom Jesus taught were strongly influenced by their religion and NOT the truths by which Jesus taught. As you read the recollections by the writers, you will run across the accounts by them where Jesus tested them and they FAILED those tests. This had a reason, and that reason was to show the world, BY "Jesus" that not even his closest associates, or his "Apostles," LISTENED very well to his message, and were influenced by their upbringing and "religion." Because of this, all Jesus taught has been obscured by the mire of rituals and traditions of man's religious precepts and not the faith the Lord gave.

Note Verse 4

Came out of Africa and were not from the "east" as presumed by scholars, as the star could not "be" from the EAST if the wisemen were TRAVELING from the east. To see the "star in the east, they would have been coming from the "WEST." Since the Mediterranean Sea is to the west of Jerusalem, the "coasts" of Egypt lay west , and one of the wise men was a "Magi." An EGYPTIAN.

Note Verse 9

Bethlehem of Judah lay to the "south" of Jerusalem and the scribe wrote they saw the star to the " east " so it was accurate except that "Nazareth" lay to the north-"EAST" of Jerusalem, not straight "east." Another discovery made in the 20th century was that much evidence points to the fact Bethlehem of Zebulon WAS where Jesus was born, NOT in Bethlehem of Judah, as many have been lead to believe in. There are two sides to this story, and it is which separates truth from lie. The Bethlehem of Judah story connects Jesus to Jewish prophesy and their King David, (Jewish converts), while the Bethlehem of Zebulon links Jesus to Egyptian prophesy.

CHAPTER 3

1 In those days came John the Baptist, a cousin of Jesus, son of the Jewish priest, Zacharias, of the course of Abia and son of Elizabeth, one of the daughters of Aaron, preaching in the wilderness of Judea,

2 Proclaiming, "Repent, for the kingdom of heaven is at hand."

3 Written in the Hebrew book of Isaiah states, "The voice of one crying in the wilderness, Prepare ye the way of the Lord, make his paths straight."

4 John, had his raiment of camel's hair, and a leathern girdle about his loins, and his meat was locusts and wild honey.

5 Many from Jerusalem, all of Judea, and all the regions round about Jordan, went out to him,

6 And were baptized by him at the Jordan river, confessing their sins.

7 But when he saw many of the Pharisees and Sadducees come to his baptism, he said unto them, "O generation of vipers, who has warned you to flee from the wrath to come?

8 Bring forth therefore fruits as a gift unto repentance,

9 And think not to say within yourselves, We have Abraham to our father, for I say unto you, that the Lord, Amen-Ra, is able of these stones to raise up children unto Abraham.

10 Now the ax is laid upon the trunk of the trees and every tree which does not bring forth good fruit is cut down, and cast into the fire.

11 I indeed baptize you with water unto repentance, but he that is coming unto you after me, is mightier than I, whose shoes I am not worthy to fill, for he shall baptize you with the Holy Spirit, and with inspiration,

12 Whose authority will throughly purge this kingdom, and gather the faithful unto the Lord in heaven, but will destroy the unworthy in damnation."

13 Then came Jesus from Galilee to the river Jordan unto John to be baptized of him.

14 But John feeling inferior, forbid him saying, "I have need to be baptized by you, but yet you come to me?"

15 And Jesus answering said, "Suffer it to be so now, for thus it has become us to fulfill all righteousness." Then John baptized him.

16 As John baptized Jesus, immediately Jesus came straight up out of the water, and, lo, heaven opened up unto him, and saw the Holy Spirit of the Father in heaven descend upon him like a dove in a glow of light all upon him,

17 And lo, a voice was heard coming from heaven, saying, "This is my beloved Son, in whom I am well pleased."

CHAPTER 4

1 Then Jesus, was led up of the Spirit into the wilderness, to be tempted by Seth, also known as Satan, the devil.

2 Jesus, full of the holy spirit, meditated and fasted for several days whereupon he became very hungry.

3 At that time, Seth, who preyed on the weaknesses of the flesh through temptations, came up to him saying, "If you be the Son of Amen, command that these stones be made into bread."

4 Jesus answered him and said, "I taught mankind centuries ago, a person can not live by bread alone, but will receive nourishment through every word that proceedth out of the mouth of Amen."

5 Then the devil took him up into the Jerusalem, and set him up on top of the highest point of the temple,

6 And said to Jesus, "If you be the Son of Amen, throw yourself from off this place, for it is written that your Father will give you authority over the angels of heaven to protect you, and into their hands will you fall, unless you doubt they will save you."

7 Jesus answered, "It is also written, Do not tempt the Lord."

8 Again, Seth took him up unto a very high mountain this time, and showed him all the kingdoms of the world, and the glory of them,

9 And said to Jesus, "I will give you all these things, if you will fall and bow down and worship me."

10 Then Jesus replied, "Get away from me Seth, you who are called Satan by the world, worship my father in heaven, your creator, and serve his will."

11 Having heard Jesus, the devil left him, and, behold, the angels of heaven came down and ministered unto him.

12 Having defeated the temptations of Seth, Jesus came out of the wilderness and heard his cousin John had been thrown into prison, so he left Jerusalem and went to see his family in Galilee,

13 On the third day after he arrived, there was a marriage in Cana of Galilee, and the mother of Jesus was invited,

14 And so was Jesus and the disciples who followed him.

15 At the wedding, they wanted wine, but the mother of Jesus said, "They don't have any wine."

16 Jesus then said to Mary, his mother, "Woman, what have I to do with you?, my hour has not come yet."

17 His mother told the servants, "What ever Jesus asks you for, do it."

18 There at the house where the wedding was taking place were six water pots of stone, used for purification purposes.

19 So Jesus asked the servants to fill the water pots with water and they filled up with water to the brim.

20 Afterwards, Jesus told them to take some out and present a drink to the governor of the feast, and did as he asked.

21 When the one giving the feast drank from the cup he'd been presented with, he asked the servants to summon unto him the bridegroom.

22 He proceeded to tell the bridegroom, "Every man at the beginning, sets out the best wine for the people to drink until it runs out, then they set out the worse wine for people to drink, but you have kept even better wine for the last. But only the servants and disciples of Jesus knew that he had changed the water into wine.

23 This was the beginning of miracles of Jesus, this one done in Cana of Galilee, which revealed his glory even more unto his disciples.

24 Leaving Nazareth in Galilee, he went and stayed in Capernaum, which is on the coast of the Mediterranean Sea, where they stayed a few days.

25 Which brings to mind what Isaiah, the Hebrew prophet wrote in his book about Jesus,

26 "The land of Zebulon, and the land of Nephthalim, by the way of the sea, beyond Jordan, Galilee of the Gentiles,   (*Note* in Index)

27 The people which sat in darkness saw great light, and to them which sat in the region and shadow of death light is sprung up."

28 Here on the coast, Jesus began to preach, proclaiming as John, "Repent, for the kingdom of heaven is at hand."

29 One day, while Jesus was walking by the sea of Galilee, he saw two brothers, Simon, who was given the name of Peter, and Andrew his brother, casting a net into the sea, for they were fishermen.

30 Jesus said to them, "Follow me, and I will make you fishers of men."

31 At that moment, they left their nets, and followed him.

32 Leaving this place, along the way Jesus saw two more brothers, James and John in a ship with their father, Zebedee, mending their nets, and called out to them.

33 Immediately they left the ship and their father, and followed him.

34 Jesus, Peter, Andrew, James and John went throughout all regions of Galilee teaching in the Jewish synagogues, preaching the gospel of the kingdom of heaven, healing all kinds of sicknesses and different diseases which afflicted the peoples.

35 Wasn't long before fame went throughout all of Syria, bringing unto Jesus all the sick peoples that were afflicted with severe diseases and their ailments even those possessed with devils, those mentally ill, those with disabling palsies, and Jesus healed them all.

36 Great multitudes of peoples began to follow him from Galilee, Decapolis, Jerusalem, Judea, and from beyond the Jordan river.

Note Verse 26

One of the most obvious facts overlooked by just about everybody who reads the New Testament, is this verse. **"GALILEE OF THE GENTILES."** A "place" Jesus was raised at and chose to "live" in. "Nazareth." To this day, anyone who knows the ethnicity of the peoples of Nazareth, can tell you that it has a strong "Arab," not "Jewish" culture. Why would the "Jewish" messiah be brought up and "live" in a place that to this day Jewish faithful deny he WAS? THEIR "messiah?" Jewish faithful in this day and age ARE those descendants of the peoples who LIVED during the time Jesus was on earth and despite all that has been deceptively written within the Roman Catholic and Christian Churches and Judeo-Christian doctrines, there is no better authorities on Jesus than those who are JEWISH.

*Note from Amen John I about Chapter 5

Within this Chapter are "attitudes" and "behaviors" given to mankind by Jesus, now referred to as the "Beattitudes," more "properly," what mankind should strive to "BE" in their lives in attitude and behavior. Because it is evident religion has had a hand on what was written by the translators, some of the submissive changes have been altered to psychologically give as much TRUTH to all Jesus taught originally. As faithful, we deal with "two" realities, the one of the "flesh" and the one of the "spirit." AS those FAITHFUL disciplines of the flesh many times have to be defended FOR the spirit of holiness over evil behaviors and it is irrational to assume goodness can have presidence over evil in the world by allowing it to destroy all that is holy. Christianity has it's roots in the Roman Empire which infected the doctrines of Jesus with many subjugatory and submissive behaviors to benefit it's rule over Jesus' faithful. Jesus was no "wimp" and his attitude in the market place and in his confrontation with leaders of the Jewish religion proves that. THIS FAITH, is as it was in the beginning where good does not lay down to evil and the Lord BEING of the spirit, "understands" mankind deals with many issues of the "flesh," which can not be ignored or "avoided." The Judeo-Christian doctrines were created "by" and "for" imperialistic dominance over peoples by Rome and it Church and have little to do with the truths Jesus taught. In the spirit of Amen, like the Pharaoh Ahmose I, Jesus taught that we should oppose unrighteousness and not lay down to it. That example came, when he was "murdered" for standing up to authorities of his time. Like the subjugatory doctrines put out by Rome to control the masses who threatened their rule by the TRUE faithful of Jesus, not many who call themselves Christians to this day have bothered to see that for about 250 years Roman leaders went after eraticating each and everyone who followed the "real" doctrines Jesus taught. If evil is to END in the flesh, it will not be done by "allowing" evil to rule even in the old doctrines put out by an evil Empire and it's church. In today's world, many still believe that these wimpy attributes belonged to the divine child sent to earth, but in his own words, it can best said. Jesus said, "He came not to bring peace, but a SWORD." We are not to seek violence or it's evil ways, but we are not to lay down to it, either.

CHAPTER 5

1 Seeing the multitude of peoples eager to hear his word, Jesus climbed up on high so the peoples could see and hear him on the mountain, and when he was ready, all the disciples came unto him.

2 As he began to speak, he taught them, saying,

3 "Blessed are the poor in spirit, for my message of heaven is for them,

4 Blessed are they that mourn, for they shall be comforted,

5 Blessed are the meek, for they shall inherit the earth,

6 Blessed are they which hunger and thirst after righteousness, for the Lord will fill them with the holy spirit,

7 Blessed are the merciful, for they shall obtain mercy,

8 Blessed are the faithful pure in heart for they will see the Lord in heaven,

9 Blessed are the peacemakers, they shall be called the children of the Lord,

10 Blessed are they who are persecuted for righteousness' sake, for theirs is the kingdom of heaven.

11 Blessed are you, when mankind reviles you, persecute you, and says all kinds of evil things against you falsely for my sake, rather,

12 Pray and rejoice, and be extremely happy, for great is your reward in heaven, for you are not the first, nor the last child of the Lord who suffers in righteousness, and the Father in heaven is just, for,

13 You are the salt of the earth. What would happen if you lose the inspiration to inspire others with the taste of heaven and grace? You would be good for nothing , for as 'salt' you would have lost your savor, to be stepped on as one who is weak,

14 You are the light of the world, so be like a city that sits on top of a hill lit at night that can't hide,

15 Just as when persons light a candle, they don't put it under a bushel, but put it on a candle holder so it will give off it's light so everyone can see with it within the house.

16 Let your inspiration, shine a light before everyone, that they may see your good works, and glorify he who gives you grace which is your Father in heaven.

17 Don't think that I have come to destroy the disciplines of your laws within your religions, for I have come to fulfill them, righteously with the wisdom of the Lord in heaven.

18 For Amen-Ra says to tell you, Until heaven and earth exist no more, not one word nor one command will change from religious laws of good for I came to fulfill them by correcting their misconceptions with truths.

19 Who ever breaks one of these least commandments, or entices another to break them, encourages bad behaviors within their faith and will be called the least in the kingdom of heaven, but who ever follows their wisdom for good and teach compassionate doctrines to others, the same shall be called great in the kingdom of heaven, for no person who lives in the flesh is perfect.

20 I am telling you, unless your behaviors and attitudes change to exceed those of some of the ones who call themselves your leaders, holy and yet can not adhere to righteousness, then you under no circumstance, will stand a chance to enter into kingdom of heaven, just as they won't.

21 You have heard it said by many of religion, God said not to kill, for those who kill will be judge by him,

22 But I say to you, Whosoever is angry with anyone without a just cause, is in danger of judgment already, for hatred leads to violence, and violence to murder, and MURDER condoned by anyone, leads to eternal damnation.

23 Therefore, if you bring a gift to your altar, and while there remember that there is someone whom you have angered or offended somewhere,

24 Leave your gift before the altar, and go to first be reconciled with that person or persons, and then come and offer your gift unto the Lord.

25 Make amends with all your enemies as quickly as possible, trying to remember all those you have offended or hurt, unless at anytime in the future one of them comes and punishes you for it. Forgive, that the Lord may forgive you.

26 For Amen-Ra says to tell you, You should by no means escape your behaviors

nor attitudes, past or present, until you have made amends for them and paid the price of reconciliation, especially to those you have hurt in your past.

27 You have heard it said by many of religion, You should not commit adultery,

28 I say to you, Whosoever looks upon a man or woman to lust after them, subjects themselves to the weakness of impure thought and it's ignorance's.

29 If you have a behavior you have a problem with, pluck it out of your life, and cast it out of your life, if need be with the help of prayer and someone of the Lord able to help. It is profitable for you to rid yourself of bad behaviors and attitudes, than to allow them to fester and ruin other graces the Father in heaven has bestowed upon your life. The Father works through all those you seek who are his faithful.

30 Is it not better to rid yourself of those things that have kept you from the kingdom of heaven, than to allow them to drag you back into damnation?

31 It has been said, Who ever puts away his wife or husband, let them give the other a divorce decree,

32 But I say to you, Who ever puts away his wife or husband, let it be for a just reason of incompatibility for we strive for perfection of the spirit and not perfection in the flesh.

33 Again, You have heard it said by many of religion, You should not make promises you can't keep, but should keep those made to the Lord,

34 But I say to you, Don't make vows nor promises you can't keep, especially to those in heaven, for it is Amen's throne,

35 Nor make them on earth, or about anything upon it, for it is his footstool.

36 Don't swear anything upon your own head, because you can't even make one hair upon it white or black.

37 Let your communication with others be simple, answering them with, Yes, yes, or No, No, where appropriate, for too much talk leads to evil.

38 You have heard it said, An eye for an eye, and a tooth for a tooth, don't resist evil, and if someone hits you on the right cheek, turn to them the other, but,

39 I say to you, tolerate evil only if it will hurt you or others to resist, be tolerant of

the ignorant and their behaviors in humility when possible. We are of the Lord, and not of a weak Father. Turn to authorities for resolve, but if evil does not listen to your humility the price is of it's own choices.

40 If any man sues you through the law and it's courts, and takes away your possess-ions without just cause, the Lord shall make it right when you seek one of the Lord's own to do the same to them in a court of law.

41 Whoever compels you to go a mile, discern the asker, for the devil has his own and he along with his angels are always trying to rob you of the Lord's blessings,

42 Give to them that ask, being careful not to be lead into a snare of the devil. Discern that which you earn and give with the heart of the Lord to those in sincere need. The ungodly have choosen their paths, and you will know their ways.

43 You have heard it said, You should love your neighbor and hate your enemies?

44 I say to you, Avoid your enemies, bless them that curse you, do good to them who hate you, and pray for them you find living without the Lord, and for those who persecute you seek the might of the Lord for resolve.

45 That you may be the children of your Father who is in heaven, for he makes his Sun to rise on hose who are evil and those who are good, and sends rain on the just and on the unjust.

46 For if you love them which only love you, what kind of example of mine will you be? Doesn't the average person out on the street act in this manner?

47 And if you salute only your brethren, will you be acting any differently than anyone else? Isn't this the way that people act out in public?

48 Try to present yourself as an example for others to follow in behavior and attitude and unto the Lord in heaven.

49 Perfection in the flesh is not a choice for the faithful, for we live amidst those of Seth and his world.

50 For those who convert unto the Lord in heaven, strive unto the perfection of the spirit in righteous behaviors and attitudes which in turn will become part of your fleshly existence.

51 You have heard me say to turn the other cheek but not unto those who are the

possessed of Seth. If evil flourish at the cost of the righteous how can the righteous flourish on earth or those of the Lord, be able to live in peace?

52 Defend the innocent, widows and children. They are the future of the Lord's kingdom, and only as a last resort against evil ways.

53 Do not immerse yourself in the love of violence, murder, drunkeness, drugs, or ways which will affect your mind and the spirit within you.

54 Evil ways are of Seth and these kind deserve punishment and damnation from those in the world for they have chosen to exist unrighteously.

55 None of the faithful should ever bow to the devil or his own, but we should not love the excuse of unrighteous living either, just to live in evil ways.

56 Practice love, use it, share it, work hard and live a sober lifestyle. Love the Lord and love each other. Inhumane disciples of Seth always pay a price.

CHAPTER 6

1 Beware that you don't give your alms before others simply to be seen of them, otherwise you will get no reward from your Father in heaven.

2 When you do give alms, don't draw attention to yourself in doing so as the hypocrites do in synagogues, temples, churches and in public, that they may gain vain glory from those they draw attention from, for Amen-Ra says to tell you, they won't be in heaven to gain a reward.

3 But when you do give, don't keep track of the amount you give or put a limit on what is given, rather,

4 Keep your alms a secret even to yourself that the Father in heaven is the only one who knows and rewards you openly.

5 When you pray, don't be like the hypocrites, for they love to pray standing in their places of worship and in public so as to draw attention unto themselves. For Amen-Ra says to tell you, they won't be in heaven to gain a reward.

6 But YOU, when you pray to the Father in heaven, do it in secret, alone and by yourself, somewhere, that your Father in heaven sees it and hears it thus rewarding you openly.

7 When you do pray, don't use vain repetitions as the heathens do, for they like to draw attention unto themselves by constant repetitions of the same words over and over again. The Lord is not "deaf," nor is he ignorant.

8 So don't be like them, for your Father in heaven knows your needs, even before you even ask him.

9 If you are going to pray, pray in this manner, **Our Father who art in heaven, Hallowed be thy name,**

10 **Thy kingdom come, Thy will be done, on earth, as it is in heaven,**

11 **Give us this day, our daily bread,**

12 **And forgive our trespasses, as we forgive those who trespass against us,**

13 **And lead us not into temptation, but deliver us from evil, for thine is the kingdom, the power, and the glory forever, Amen.**

14 If you forgive persons their trespasses, your heavenly Father will also forgive you, but if you refuse to forgive anyone how can you expect your Father in heaven to forgive you?

15 Evil ones will use this against you, but you are wise enough to know who are the worthy of this gift and who are not.

16 When you decide to fast, don't be like the hypocrites, sad, disfiguring your face so everyone around you will know that you are fasting, for Amen-Ra says to tell you, they won't be in heaven to gain a reward. Do it for discipline.

17 But you, when you fast, anoint your head, wash your face, so

18 That you will not appear unto others to fast, but only unto your Father who sees your discipline over the flesh in secret and rewards you openly.

19 Lay not treasures up for yourselves unrighteously, through behaviors of lust and greed or using others for a life of prosperity and wealth.

20 But rather give thanks to the Lord for your blessings and give unto the less fortunate in the flesh that they may see your spirit and be the example in faith unto themselves and others,

21 Where your treasure is, there will your heart be also,

22 The light of the body is your intellect, if therefore your thinking is righteous, your whole body shall be full of light for the flesh will follow the intellect of your spirit.

23 But if use your intellect for evil, you will be of evil deeds and thoughts, for all righteousness in you is overcome by those evil deeds and thoughts,

24 No one can serve two Masters, for either he will hate one, and love the other, or else be obsessed with one and and despise the other. You cannot do the things of the Lord in heaven while obsessed with material wealth and the evils of this world,

25 Therefore I say to you, Life is to be enjoyed and won't be if you worry over every little thing in it.

26 A righteous person has confidence the Lord will be there in all circumstances, and is, while evil ones lack all things for there is never enough and have confidence

in nothing, not even themselves.

27 Look upon the birds of the air, do they save up for themselves gathering their needs up in excess, storing things up for themselves in barns. If the heavenly Father has seen to their needs, aren't you much greater than they are? Wealth gained honestly is provision unto the wise who shall keep it.

28 Which of you by simply thinking it, can add height to your stature?

29 So why worry over what clothes you are going to wear? Consider the lilies of the field, how they grow, and they didn't even bother to plant themselves or worry about staying alive,

30 Yet I say to you, That even Solomon in all his glory was not as organized as one of these.

31 Wherefore, if Amen in heaven takes care of all the things he created, which tomorrow if he so wished he could cast it all into an oven, don't you think he can take care of you? Oh, those of you, of little faith?

32 Therefore the person who is righteous, faithful and responsible should take no thought about saying, "What shall we eat, or what shall we drink, or who will put clothes upon my back."

33 (For after all these things are the questions evil persons ask themselves). Your heavenly Father knows you have need of all these things and as his faithful, also care for each other that no one is found wanting.

34 Seek first the Kingdom of the Lord in heaven, living in all his righteousness, being responsible, working to better your lives and all these things will be added unto you, not of yourself, but the Lord.

35 Quit worrying about tomorrows problems, thinking on only those for the day, for tomorrow is tomorrow and it is sufficient to only think upon the Lord fulfilling your present needs.

36 Whenever you fill your lives with the thoughts of heavenly things, all that you have need of in the flesh comes from the Lord including wealth and prosperity.

37 Worry is to the unwise who squander all they take in greed unto a life they never learn to enjoy. Don't take what you do not deserve while hurting another amongst you. Live honestly, work and pray and the Lord will provide to your well being.

CHAPTER 7

1 Don't go around judging people, or else you could be judged yourself.

2 And if you do judge, with whatever amount you judge others with, so will you suffer the same judgments upon yourself.

3 Why is it that you feel you can judge what you think is wrong in the lives of another person or persons but can not see the wrong you are committing by not removing your wrong of judging them?

4 Who will say to another, "Let me help you remove what I see as wrong in your life," when they won't acknowledge what is wrong in their own?

5 You hypocrite, first cast out that bad behavior of judging others out of your own life that you can see clearly that it is not your responsibility to go around judging others.

6 Don't be giving that which is holy to those who don't deserve it, nor cast that which is sacred amongst filth for all they will do it trash it, step on it and destroy it and then they will do it to you.

7 Ask, and it shall be given you. Seek, and you will find, Knock, and it will be opened unto you. Effort is it's own reward.

8 For everyone that has faith in the Lord and lacks not confidence in themselves and asks, will receive, everyone that seeks, shall find, and if they knock, it shall be opened.

9 Which one amongst you would turn away your children if they ask for bread. Would you give them a stone?

10 Or if they ask you for a meal, will you give them a snake?

11 If you, then being evil, know how to treat your children well, how much more abundantly do you think the Father in heaven will treat the ones who are his faithful children that ask him?

12 Therefore, pay attention to what I am teaching you by this example, for in all things how ever you want others to treat you, treat them that way and also treat them with respect. You wants respect? Give others respect.

13 Many enter into religions, whose gates are wide and popular, teaching they know the ways to heaven, for they make things easy and appealing and take no effort or work to join but I tell you that their paths leads to destruction,

14 Because these gates offers no obstacles, many enter them for the gate to heaven is narrow and alot of effort to go through but I say that it is the path that leads unto life and there will be few that take it, or find it.

15 Beware of false prophets, for they come to you passively displaying a heavenly nature when in fact, they are nothing more than persons out to take advantage of those who listen to them, ruining peoples lives.

16 You will know them by the examples they have left behind, many of them the innocent who did not listen to my warning about them. People should not look to bad examples who persistently show they will not change to gain what is good. Leaders of religion whose history is full of thorns not bearing "good" fruit that will enter heaven.

17 Justly so, every good tree bears good fruit, but a corrupt tree brings forth evil fruit, and this applies in all aspects of your lives to discern the false ones who refer to themselves as "holy."

18 A good tree cannot bring forth evil fruit, just as a person of the Devil can not go out and behave like a person of the Lord in heaven. They can "act" it, but a discerning person of the Lord, will know the truth.

19 Every tree that does not bring forth good fruit, will be cut down, and cast into damnation, just as every person who subjugates the naive and ignorant.

20 Those of the Lord know them by the fruits of their deceptions, and

21 Not everyone that proclaims me that says, "Lord, Lord," will enter the Kingdom of heaven, except those who do the will of my Father in heaven.

22 In the end when they pass from this life many will say to me, "Lord, Lord, have we not prophesied in your name and in your name have we not cast out devils and in your name done many wonderful works?

23 At that time I will profess to them, "I never knew your works nor do I know who you are, so depart from my sight you vain work of iniquity."

24 Therefore whosoever hears these teachings I am giving, and does them, I will compare to the wise man who built his house upon a rock,

25 Who when the rains fell creating floods throughout, the strong winds blew fiercely upon that house, and it didn't fall, for it's foundation was upon a rock.

26 But everyone who hears these teachings I am giving, and doesn't do them, will be like the foolish man, who built his house upon sand,

27 And when the rains fell creating floods throughout, and the strong winds blew fiercely upon that house, it fell, for it's foundation was built upon sand and great was the fall of it.

28 It came to pass, that when Jesus, whom the Jewish peoples called Yeshua, was done with his sermon on the mountain, all these teachings astonished the peoples who were there and were amazed of his wisdom and his doctrines.

29 For he taught them as someone having authority, unlike that of the Jewish scribes.

CHAPTER 8

1 When he was came down from the mountain, great multitudes of peoples followed him.

2 As he descended the mountain, a leper came up to him, worshiping him, and said, "Lord, if you can, would you clean me of this leprosy."

3 And Jesus put forth his hand, touched him, and said, "I will, be thou clean." And immediately his leprosy was cleansed.

4 Then Jesus told him, "Go your own way and see to it that you don't tell anyone except to show yourself to the priests as a testimony unto them."

5 Jesus then left to Capernaum and when he entered there, a centurion came up to him desperate for help,

6 Saying, "Lord, my servant is at home in bed very sick with the palsy, grievously tormented.

7 So Jesus comforted him and said, "I will come and heal him."

8 Then the centurion humbly feeling inferior said, "Lord, I am not worthy that you should even step into my home, speak the word only, so that my servant may be healed.

9 For I am a man of authority being the commanding officer of soldiers who are under my direction and whatever I command them or my servants to do, they have to follow my orders, yet I be 'your' servant if you would do this one thing for me."

10 When Jesus heard this, he marveled, and said to them that followed, "For Amen-Ra says to tell you, he has not found so great a faith, No, not in all Israel, of which to this day thinks their faith is of the Lord in heaven.

11 Many shall come from the east and many shall come from the west, and shall sit down in their synagogues with their prophets books of Abraham, Isaac, and Jacob, declaring they do it for the kingdom of heaven,

12 But the children of THAT kingdom (the Jewish faith) shall be cast out into outer darkness, for they do not know how to humble themselves as you have done before me, and to those who know not humility, will suffer weeping and the

gnashing of teeth, of such are those of these prophets faith."

13 Then Jesus said to the centurion, "Go on home to see that your servant has been healed this minute by that of your humility and your devout faith."

14 After this, Jesus went to visit Peter at his house. As he entered he noticed that his wife's mother was in bed sick with a bad fever.

15 As he touched her hand, the fever immediately left her, whereupon she arose, ministering to those in the house.

16 That evening, they brought to him many that were possessed with devils, casting out the spirits with his word, and also healing many who were sick,

17 Everywhere he went, there were people who needed his attention and by now Jesus was growing weary,

18 When he saw great multitudes of people around him, he ordered that they depart and find a way to get to where he had to go amongst the Gergesenes, if they could, since he would be ministering there.

19 Thinking it an invitation, a certain scribe came before him and said, "Master, I will follow you wherever you go."

20 And Jesus told him, "Foxes have holes, and birds of the air have nests, but the Son of man doesn't even have a place to lay his head."

21 Growing even more tired, another of his disciples asked, "Lord, before you rest could you do me the favor first of helping me to bury my father."

22 But Jesus said to him, "Follow me, and let the dead bury their dead."

23 That night they set sail for the country of the Gergesenes, and as he boarded the ship, his disciples who were to go with him, followed him.

24 Along the way, behold, a great tempest arose from the sea, one so bad that the ship was swaying back nd forth, engulfed by all the waves, yet Jesus, had been so tired that the tempest did not wake him from his sleep.

25 Scared by the storm, his disciples went and woke him up and exclaimed, "Lord, why don't you save us before we all perish."

26 And he said to them, "Why are you so scared, do you lack that much faith as to fear for your life while I am here?" Then he got up, and calmed the winds and the

sea, to where the storm just disappeared.

27 When the disciples saw this, they mumbled to themselves, saying, "What manner of man is this, that even the winds and the sea obey him?"

28 The next day when they reached their destination of the country of the Gergesenes, they disembarked the vessel and began to walk towards a community and were met by two persons who were possessed by devils coming out of some tombs, looking exceeding fierce and mean that they would not let anyone pass by that way.

29 In a loud voice, they cried out saying, "What have we done to you Jesus, Son of Amen? Have you come here to torment us before the time?"

30 In a field in the distance from them was a herd of pigs, eating.

31 Seeing the pigs, the devils begged of him, saying, "If you cast us out of these persons would you at least cast us into the herd of swine in the distance?"

32 Jesus answered them, "Go.", and when they came out they went into the herd of pigs, and at that moment, the whole herd of swine ran violently down a steep ledge and jumped into the sea, and perished in the waters.

33 And those who owned the pigs immediately ran, heading towards the city telling everybody they met what had just happened and how Jesus had cleansed the persons possessed of the devils.

34 When the peoples heard this, the whole city came out to meet Jesus, and when they saw one of the ones that had been possessed by the devils, begged him to leave their country, for they were afraid.

35 Then the man asked Jesus if he could come with him, but Jesus said to the man that his place was with his family and he should go home.

CHAPTER 9

1 As Jesus boarded the ship, they set sail back to the coasts of Galilee where they went into his hometown of Nazareth, the land of Gentiles.

2 Not long after arriving there they brought to him a man who was sick with palsy, lying on a cot. Jesus seeing the faith of the peoples around him said, to the man sick of the palsy, "Son, don't be depressed, be happy for your sins are forgiven."

3 Just then, certain scribes in the midst of the crowd, thought to themselves, 'This man is a blasphemer.'

4 But Jesus knowing their thoughts, let it be known that he knew them and replied, "Wherefore do you think evil of me in your hearts?

5 For which would you agree is easier for me to say, "Your sins be forgiven, or Arise!, and walk?

6 But I said this so you will know, that the Son of man has the power on earth to forgive sins." Then Jesus said to the man he had just healed of palsy, "Arise, pick up your cot, and go home."

7 And he got up, took his cot and left.

8 When the multitude of peoples around him saw it, they were astounded and marveled, glorifying the Lord in heaven, who gave Jesus such power to heal.

9 As Jesus walked the streets of Nazareth, he saw a man, whose name was Matthew, sitting at the receipt of customs. Looking at the man, he said, "Follow me." Matthew got up, and followed him.

10 Later on as Jesus sat down at a house to eat, surprisingly, alot of known troublemakers in the community and people known to be unrighteous, sat down with him and his disciples.

11 When the Pharisees saw this, they said to his disciples, "Why does your Master sit down to eat with these degenerates?"

12 Jesus heard this, and said to them, "Those who are not sick, don't need a Physician, but thosewho need one, seek one that can heal them.

13 Go and find out the meaning of what I have just told you, for I don't give sacri-

fice to atone for sin, but give mercy, for I haven't come to call the righteous to learn of Amen, but those who need to change their behaviors, and their ways as to repent for them.

14 Then came the disciples of his cousin John up to him, saying, "Why don't you and your disciples keep to the tradition of fasting as written. We, as well as the Pharisees, obey our traditions, why don't you?

15 Jesus answered them, "Can the children of the bride's chamber mourn the loss of the bridegroom, if that bridegroom is still amongst them? The day will come when he will no longer be amongst them as he will be taken from them. Then they will have to discipline themselves, if by fasting, only then.

16 Nobody mends a useless old garment with a new piece of cloth, for it will look ridiculous for the new cloth will stand out upon the old and make the whole garment look worse.

17 You don't see people pouring new wine in old bottles, simply because the old bottles will break from the pressure and the wine would perish. Instead, they put the new wine in new bottles so the wine will stay preserved."

18 While he was speaking to the disciples of John, a certain ruler came worshiping him, saying, "My daughter is dead and even though she is, would you come and lay your hands upon her, that she may rise and live."

19 Jesus rose from his seat, as did the disciples, following the ruler to his home.

20 On the way there, a woman who for twelve years was ill with a feminine blood disorder came up behind him and touched the hem of his garment.

21 For in faith, she thought to herself, for if I may but touch his garment, I will be healed.

22 But Jesus, noticed her as she came up behind him and turned around and said, "Daughter, be happy, for your faith is what has healed you." And the woman was healed that very same moment.

23 Returning along the way to the ruler's house, Jesus saw the minstrels and heard them playing music and singing,

24 Just then, he said to them, "Move aside so I may see the girl, for she isn't dead.

She's just sleeping." Hearing this, they scornfully laughed at him.

25 After these people were moved aside, Jesus went in and took the girl by the hand and she arose from amongst the dead.

26 And his fame from here on out went abroad and throughout the land.

27 As Jesus was departing the ruler's home, two blind men followed him crying, saying, "Oh, Son of Amen, have mercy upon us."

28 Coming out of the house, the blind men came up to him, and Jesus asked them, "Do you believe that I am able to do that which you are asking of me to do?" They replied. "Yes Lord."

29 Then he touched their eyes, stating, "According to your faith be it so done unto you."

30 And immediately they received sight and were able to see Jesus in front of them. Jesus sternly told them, "See that you tell nobody about this."

31 But they, being overjoyed, departed, and spread about his fame throughout even more so.

32 As they were walking, some people brought to Jesus a man who didn't speak, possessed by a devil.

33 Laying his hands upon him, Jesus castout the devil and he came out of the man that instant whereupon the man began to talk again praising Jesus, that all the peoples who saw it were so amazed that it was said that such miracles have never been seen in all of Israel.

34 By then, though, the Pharisees casted doubt upon all Jesus did proclaiming and saying amongst themselves, "Jesus was casting out devils through the prince of the devils, himself."

35 Not paying attention to all the doubters, Jesus went about all the cities and villages, teaching in their synagogues, preaching the gospel of the kingdom of Amen, healing many illnesses and every kind of diseases that afflicted the peoples.

36 When he saw how many needed his help, he was moved with compassion for them, because he could see that the waiting was hard on so many, and many

fainted from being so weak, and most were coming to him from far away that they were lost to their surroundings.

37 Then Jesus said to his disciples, "There are so many who need our help, but so few of us to do the work that's before us.

38 Pray to the Lord in heaven that he will send us more disciples who will be able to help us with these faithful children.

CHAPTER 10

1 Overwhelmed with his tasks, Jesus summoned his twelve disciples and gave them power to exorcise unclean spirits, and to heal all kinds of illness and disease that afflicted the peoples.

2 The names of the twelve apostles chosen by Jesus were, Simon, who also went by the name of Peter, Andrew, his brother, James and John, brothers, sons of Zebedee,

3 Phillip, Bartholomew, Thomas, Levi who was a tax collector who went by the name of Matthew and his brother James, both sons of Alphaeus, and Lebbaeus, whose surname was Thaddeus.

4 Simon, the Canaanite, and Judas Iscariot. In the court of Amen, "council" consists of twelve in the flesh, in accordance to the 12 Gods (angels) closest to the Lord.

5 It was these twelve, Jesus sent out amongst the peoples, commanding them, saying, "Don't go amongst the gentiles, or any cities of the Samaritans, yet,

6 But rather go amongst the lost sheep of the house of Israel.

7 And as you go amongst the house of Israel, preach, proclaiming unto them, "The kingdom of heaven is at hand.

8 Heal the sick and diseased, cleanse the lepers, raise the dead, and cast out devils, just as freely as you have received, freely give unto others.

9 Don't take with you gold, silver, or brass in your purses for money,

10 Or paper to write on for your journey. Don't even take two coats, shoes, or staffs with you. Earn what you need, by working for it.

11 In what ever city or town you happen to enter, inquire who is a disciple and ask one of them to let you stay the duration of your visit.

12 When you come into their house, bless it.

13 And if those in the house are worthy disciples, let your peace be upon the house they dwell in, if they are not worthy, leave.

14 And whoever does not receive you in any house or that city does not want to accept what you have to teach them, don't bother with them.

15 For Amen-Ra says to tell you, "The judgment their God took on Sodom and Gomorrah isn't as bad as the one he will take against them.

16 I send you out as sheep amidst wolves, so be diligent that you are much wiser than they are and just as shrewd, but harmless as doves.

17 Beware of those people who will arrest you or deliver you before those of authority degrading you and putting you down in their synagogues, temples and churches, for

18 You will also be taken before governors, kings and emperors for your faith in me and the Father in heaven but what they do to you will be a testimony against them.

19 If and when they deliver you before any of these kind of persons, don't worry or give thought about what to do or say, for in that instant you will receive the spirit of wisdom in what to say and do.

20 For it won't be you doing the talking, it will be the Spirit of your Father in heaven who will enter you at that moment.

21 For brother will turn against brother, sister against sister, parents against their own children, just as children will turn against their own parents, and cause them to be put to death.

22 And you will be hated by everyone for your faith, but the person who endures how they are treated, even unto death, will be saved.

23 Be wise, therefore as to see that if they persecute you in any particular city or house, flee to another, for Amen-Ra says to tell you, you will not have gone into all the cities of the world before you see me again.

24 A disciple is not above an apostle, nor are any of them above the Lord.

25 It is enough that every person should treat each other as an equal, just as the Lord treats all his children equally. If they call the Devil their Master, how can people respect or treat each other on the same level of dignity if their nature is the same as their Master?

26 Don't be afraid of these kinds of peoples, for they aren't of our nature and blind to their own and you will see it by the way they behave, and in their attitudes to-

wards others, a nature, you are wise enough to see through.

27 What I am teaching you about the ways of darkness, teach it to others with all I have taught you about living in the wisdoms of heaven, and do so wherever you happen to be.

28 Don't be scared of those who can kill the body, and can't kill the soul, but fear being deceived by the devil who is able to destroy both body and soul in hell and in his deceptive religions on earth.

29 Are not two sparrows sold for a farthing?, yet neither one of them will die without your Father knowing about it.

30 The days of your own life are like the hairs on your head, for they are all numbered.

31 So don't be afraid, you are more valuable than any sparrow.

32 Whosoever teaches others of all I have taught and that I am the Son of Amen-Ra in heaven, that person will I confess before my Father who is in heaven.

33 But whosoever denies I am of the spirit and flesh, Son of Amen and Son of Man, through Mary my mother, that person will I also deny before my Father who is in heaven.

34 Don't think that I was born of the flesh and it will bring peace upon the earth, for I was born to bring truth in it which will drive a wedge between people whose vain nature will not accept it.

35 I have come, and the truth will set many sons against their fathers, daughters against their mothers, and daughter-in-laws against their mother-in-laws.

36 And it will not be unusual for a person's worse enemies, to be the very members of their own households.

37 A person that loves family members, more, than they love my teachings and following them, is not worthy of me or the kingdom of heaven.

38 The person who doesn't adhere to my teachings and helps others no matter who they be, is not worthy of me.

39 A person who vainly is obsessed with life and the things of it, will lose it, but the person who is obsessed with doing the things I teach about and loses their

life in the process, will gain it in heaven.

40 The persons who receive you into their lives, receive me, and the Father in heaven who sent me.

41 For those who receive a prophet in the name of a prophet, will receive a prophet's reward, and those who receive a righteous person in the name of a another righteous person, will receive a righteous person's reward.

42 And whoever gives a cup of cold water to drink to anyone of these little ones of faith in the name of a disciple, Amen-Ra says to tell you, will for no reason lose their reward."

CHAPTER 11

1 And after Jesus finished instructing his chosen twelve apostles, he sent them on their way and departed, himself, to teach and preach in various cities of Israel.

2 When his cousin, John the Baptist, heard in prison about the works of his cousin Jesus, the next time his disciples came to see him, he asked that two of them go see if it was true.

3 When the two disciple found Jesus, they ask him, "Are you the chosen one that it is written about, cousin to our prophet, or are we mistaken?"

4 Jesus answered them and said, "Go to my cousin who sits in prison and be witnesses unto him of the things you see and hear me do,

5 The blind receive their sight, the lame walk, lepers are cleansed, the deaf hear, the dead rise up, and the poor have the words of the Lord in heaven preached unto them.

6 And blessed are those who are not offended by me or by the works, the Father in heaven has bestowed upon me to do,

7 As the disciples of John left, his cousin Jesus departed and began to speak to the multitude of peoples surrounding him concerning John, exclaiming, "Why did you go out in the wilderness to see? A reed shaking in the wind?

8 No. What did you see, a man dressed up in fine clothes that are worn only by the rich or those in king's houses or eating the finest foods?

9 No. What did you go out to see? A prophet? That's what you saw, wasn't it, a mere man, a prophet of God in heaven who was much more than a prophet.

10 For this is the person of whom it is written in your books that states, 'Behold, I send my messenger before thy face, which shall prepare thy way before you.'

11 Amen-Ra says to tell you, Amongst them that are born of women, there hasn't been one born yet who is a greater person than John the Baptist, but not meaning to be condescending, even the least important one in heaven is more important than John.

12 From the very day John the Baptist was born up to now, the kingdom of heaven

suffers violence, for in this world the violent take it by force.

13 For all the ancient prophets and I was prophesied up until he was born.

14 And if you are willing to accept it, this is the one foretold would come by your prophet, Isaiah, having heard it of followers of the Book of Ani.

15 For the person who is not deaf to the truth, will hear these words.

16 But how can I compare this generation to? It is like children sitting in the market places, calling out to the people passing by,

17 Saying, 'We have played music for you, and you have not danced, cried and you have not felt sorry for us,'

18 My cousin, John, came amongst you not even being a drunk or a glutton, yet many exclaim that he is possessed by a devil.

19 The Son of man came amongst you also not being a drunk or a glutton, and many of you say, Look at this gluttonous man, a drunk, a friend of those officials of the state and sinners. Wisdom is justified by her children."

20 Then Jesus began to criticize many cities he had visited for he was ashamed that though he had mighty works in them the peoples did not repent.

21 "Woe to you, Chorazin! Woe to you, Bethsaida! For if I had done the mighty works I did in your cities in Tyre and Sidon, they would have repented long ago in sackcloth and ashes.

22 But I am telling you, It will be more tolerable for Tyre and Sidon on the day of judgment, than it will be for you.

23 And you, Capernaum, which are exalted unto heaven, will be brought down to hell, for if the mighty works which have been done in your city had been done in Sodom, Sodom would presently exist.

24 But I am telling you, It will be more tolerable for the land of Sodom on the day of judgment, than it will be for you."

25 At that moment, Jesus prayed out loud for the peoples in those cities who would not repent, "I thank you, Father, Lord of heaven and earth, because you have hid these things from the wise and prudent and have revealed them unto your faithful.

26 Even so, Father, though it seems good in your sight.

27 All these things are delivered unto me by you to do, that no man knows that who I really am except you, nor does any person know that you are Amen-Ra, except me and those you have given unto me to reveal your truths.

28 For them I ask to, Come unto me, all of you that work hard and are burdened by the cares of this world, and I will give you rest.

29 Take my mission upon you, and learn of me, for I am meek and passive in nature and compassionate in heart, for you will find rest unto your souls.

30 For my mission is easy, and my burden, light."

CHAPTER 12

1 The following sabbath, Jesus and the disciples were all hungry whereupon they came upon a field where corn was being grown. Going out into the field, Jesus began to pluck some of the ears of corn, to eat.

2 Some men who were Pharisees saw what they were doing and yelled out to them, and said, "Behold, why do you and your disciples do that which is unlawful to do upon the sabbath day?"

3 Jesus answered, "Have you not read what your King David, along with those who were with him did one day when they too were hungry?

4 They entered in the house of your God, and ate from the unleavened bread which was unlawful for them to do also, for the bread was not for them but was only for the priests of the temple.

5 Even so, haven't you read your own laws? How is it that on days of the sabbath, priests profane this day by eating in the temple, yet none of you are held accountable for your actions?

6 I say to you, That you stand before a greater temple than your own,

7 For if you knew what this meant, I would give you mercy for your ignorant accusations, not sacrifice, as you are accustom to giving. You also wouldn't go around condemning those who have done nothing wrong.

8 For the Son of man standing before you, is Lord, even, of the sabbath day."

9 When Jesus and his disciples left, the Pharisees followed as they went in the direction of the synagogue, and Jesus went in.

10 As Jesus walked inside, behold, there was a man who had a hand that was withered, so the Pharisees, seeing a chance to accuse him of doing wrong again asked him, "Is it lawful to heal on the day of the sabbath?

11 To which Jesus replied, "What man amongst you that has a sheep fall into a pit on the sabbath day won't bother to fetch it out of that pit and lift it out?

12 Isn't a man worth more than sheep? Then I say it is lawful to good things on any day, including the sabbath."

13 Then he looked at the man with the withered hand and said, "Stretch out your hand to me." And the man stretched it out to Jesus, where he touched it and it was immediately healed, just like the man's other one.

14 Seeing this, the Pharisees soon left and convened a council against Jesus to discuss how they could rid themselves of him.

15 When Jesus found out about this, he left that city, and great multitudes of peoples followed him until he got around to healing all of them.

16 Asking of them, only, that they keep his location a secret.

17 Later on, the peoples brought to him a man who was possessed with a devil, also blind, and could not speak and Jesus healed him. The man was able to speak and also regained his sight.

18 Seeing this, all the people were astonished, saying, "Isn't this the Son of Amen?"

19 But when the Pharisees heard this from the peoples, they said, "This person casts out devils through the powers of Beelzebub, the prince devils."

20 Not knowing that Jesus was amongst the peoples, he said to them, "Every kingdom divided against itself is brought to desolation, and every city or house divided against itself, will not stand,

21 If Seth, who is the prince of the devils, casts out his own, is he not going against those of his own kingdom?, and how would HIS kingdom stand?

22 If 'I,' by this demon Beelzebub, cast out devils, by whose power do your children cast them out? They know who Amen is, and they will be your judges.

23 But if I cast out devils by the powers of the Father in heaven, who is Amen, then the kingdom of heaven has come to you.

24 How can anybody enter a strong man's house to spoil his goods except he first bind up the strong man, then spoil his house.

25 The person who is not with me in purpose, is against me, and the person who doesn't do their part for the kingdom, lets down not only me but themselves,

26 So I am saying to you, All manner of sin and blasphemy will be forgiven of everyone where it concerns the flesh amongst you, but the blasphemy against the Holy Spirit in heaven will not be forgiven of anyone.

27 Who ever speaks a word against the Son of man, it will be forgiven him, but who ever speaks against the Holy Spirit in heaven, will not be forgiven, in heaven or on earth.

28 All of you have the powers of choice and the powers of decision. You can either choose to be good, and your rewards will be good, or you can decide to behave badly, and face the consequence for your actions. Either way, you will be judged by your behaviors.

29 Generation of vipers, how can you, being evil, speak good things? Out of the heart comes compassion not from the mouth,

30 For you will know a good person by all that they show and have accomplished, just as you will know an evil person, by their ways that accomplish only more evil.

31 I am telling you, everything a person criticizes another for, that very person will have to account for it in their day of judgment.

32 For you are the ones who choose your worthiness by your words, for it is by them that you are justified, and if not, those words will be the ones to condemn you."

33 Then certain scribes and Pharisees asked, "Master, if we are wrong will we see a sign from you that we may know you are coming?"

34 But he answered them and said, "An evil and adulterous generation seeks to be forewarned by signs to escape their punishment, but there will be no sign or signs given at that time except the sign of Jonah,

35 For as Jonah was three days and three nights in the belly of a whale, so will the Son of man be, three days and three nights in the belly of the earth.

36 The peoples of Nineveh will rise in judgment against this generation, and will condemn it, because it is willing to repent at the preaching of Jonah, but not at my own, for before you stands one greater than Jonah.

37 The queen of the south will rise up in the judgment with this generation, and will condemn it, for she came from the uttermost parts of the earth to hear the wisdom of Solomon, yet before you stands one greater than Solomon.

38 When unclean spirit is cast out of a house, it walks through the deserts seeking rest, but finds none.

39 Then it says to itself, I will return to the house from where I was cast out but upon going into the house, finds the house empty, clean, and ganished.

40 So the unclean spirit goes out and takes with it seven other spirits even more wicked than itself, and go back to that house and dwell there, and the state of anyone who enters there is worse than it was in the beginning. So will it be with this wicked generation."

41 While he was busy talking to the scribes and Pharisees, his mother and members of his family came and stood there, desiring to speak with him.

42 Then someone said, "Jesus, your mother and your family desire to speak to you."

43 But he answered the one who called upon him, "Who is my mother? Who is my family?"

44 Stretching his hand out to his disciples, he exclaimed, "Behold my mother and my family!

45 For who ever does the will of my Father in heaven, the same is my brother, sister, and mother.

46 In the Father, we are all his children and his family, though born of flesh, into the cultures of mankind and it's religions, we are all one in spirit who chose the ways of the Lord in heaven.   (*Note* in Index)

47 Those ways are in love for one another, equal in respect for one another, regardless of race, color, or creed.

48 Though we all have a mother, father, brothers or sisters of the flesh, you as disciples are also members of the family of the Lord in heaven who is spirit.

49 Don't seek only to help family of the flesh, but also family in spirit and when one is in need, do that which you would want done unto you if in the same situation.

50 For this purpose, is love given, and as it is given unto you so give unto others.

51 The unity of mankind, divides itself in hate, for one person is always set to fight with another, never considering that it has never gained peace.

52 If a person would consider to treat another like they treat themselves, love might have a chance to grow to where everyone becomes not just family in the spirit, but would treat each other as family in the 'flesh.'"

Note Verses 46-52 ;

Written by the author to supplement the teachings of Jesus. The obvious fact that has evaded the masses about all Jesus taught, is "psychological" perspectives in how we behave, we as a species were not aware of at the time. Many of those who blindly follow much of what was written within Roman doctrines and it's church or what has become known as "christianity," up until recently, neglected to acknowledge that Jesus taught personal responsibility to individuals and the steps to behavioral modifications they could take. By applying changes to their live in how they treated others, they themselves might achieve better treatment. Only in the last 20 to 30 years have ministers of christianity realized that people NEED to take an initative to be responsible psychologically to change many of their deep rooted bad habits. It is fine to have a belief the Lord gives us miracles, but if we make no effort to gain them, we will simply fail time and again because we expect him to reward us without proving ourselves worthy of it.

CHAPTER 13

1 After these teachings, Jesus went into a house but later that same day, he came out of the house, and went and sat by the sea.

2 Great multitudes of peoples gathered around him, but Jesus knowing that they yearned for more knowledge of the kingdom of heaven, boarded a ship, while the peoples stood on the shore waiting to see what he had to teach. When he was on the ship, he sat down.

3 Jesus began to speak many things to them in parables, saying, "Listen up. A farmer went out unto his field to plant some seed.

4 And while he planted, some seeds fell out of his hands by the way side, and some birds flew down and ate them.

5 Some of the seeds fell between stones, that the birds did not get them. Though there wasn't much earth there, some of those seeds grew, but because there wasn't much dirt there,

6 The sun scorched those plants, as they had no root, so they dried up.

7 Yet other seeds, fell amongst thorns, and there too, the birds could not eat those seeds, so they grew, but the other plants with thorns choked the growth of those seeds, and they too dried up.

8 But those seeds the farmer planted into firm good earth, could not be destroyed by the sun or birds and brought forth fruit, in some places a hundredfold, in others sixty fold, and yet another, thirty fold.

9 For those of you who are listening, listen well, for you will be that sower and the teachings I give you, is that seed."

10 And the disciples came, and asked him, "Why do you speak to the peoples in parables?"

11 Jesus promptly answered them, "All of you whom I have chosen to be my apostles have been given the mysteries of the kingdom of heaven, but to the peoples I am teaching, they have to 'earn' that kingdom by taking the time to figure out these parables I give them to gain it's wisdom,

12 For who ever makes the efforts to earn that wisdom, will be given even more, abundantly, and for those who don't make the efforts to figure these parables out, is not worthy of the kingdom and what little wisdom they have, they will lose.

13 Now you understand why I speak to them in parables, because though they see miracles in front of them given to them of a God, many refuse to accept them for they are blinded by their own perception of who the Lord is and what are all the ways of heaven and what is holy.

14 They also hear the truth given them of the kingdom of heaven, but many will refuse to listen to it because in their hearts they would rather believe man made holy words in ancient books than in those given by Amen,

15 Of the Hebrew prophets, Isaiah wrote of this 800 years ago when he said the very same things, concerning the peoples of his day.

16 But you, my apostles, are blessed, for you have been given insight into the holy one's celestial knowledge to see it's truth, and you can hear that wisdom because I selected you from amongst them in the world.

17 For Amen-Ra says to tell you, That many prophets and men who thought them- selves righteous men, have desired to see those things which you see, and have not seen them, and have also desired to hear those things which you hear, and will never hear them.

18 So remember what I have said here in this parable of the sower, for you are my chosen 'farmers' who will be planting that seed amongst the peoples of this world.

19 When you are preaching these words of the Lord and anyone hears but doesn't understand them, the devil comes quickly and takes away that which you have sown in their heart. This is the person who is like that seed that fell by the way side in the parable.

20 Another is the person who hears the Lord's word, accepts it with exceeding great joy, and is joyful that they have received it.

21 But these type of persons don't let the word of the Lord take root in their hearts , and will remain faithful for a while, but when life's circumstances become hard on them or people begin to persecute them because of their faith, they go back to

being just like they were before receiving their "word." These people, are like the seeds that fall amongst the stones in the parable.

22 As for the seeds that fall amongst the thorns, it is like the persons who hear the word of the Lord, use it deceitfully to make themselves rich, thus choking the word, becoming unfruitful in properly leading people into the kingdom of heaven by their false teachings for they are the blind leading the blind.

23 But a person who receives and hears the word of the Lord, understands it and goes out and does what I have taught, teaching others that they too can be saved from all their bad behaviors and the evils of this world, bringing in a hundred, sixty or thirty fold into the family of the most holy one is like the seed that falls into fertile ground and brings forth good fruit."

24 Then Jesus began to tell them another parable, saying, "The kingdom of heaven is like the person who plants good seed into the ground in a field,

25 But while that person is asleep, an enemy goes into the field and plants weeds amongst wheat planted there. The enemy then leaves.

26 When it's time to harvest the wheat and cut with the blade, it not only yields wheat, but the weeds within it as well.

27 So the servants of the owner of the field come and exclaim, 'Sir, didn't you plant good seed in your field? From where did all the weeds come from?'

28 He answered them, 'An enemy has done this.' So the servants asked him, 'Do you want us to go harvest the wheat mixed with weeds in it?'

29 But the owner said, 'No, since there will be too many weeds mixed in with the wheat.

30 When it's time to harvest the wheat we will all go out into the fields and I will tell all you reapers, first gather up the weeds in the fields and bind them together in bundles so we can burn them, then we can harvest the wheat and put it in my barn.'"

31 Jesus continued with yet another parable, saying, "The kingdom of heaven is like a grain of a mustard seed, which a farmer took and planted it in his field.

32 Though it is the smallest of all seeds, when it planted and grown, it becomes the

greatest amongst the herbs becoming a tree, so that the birds of the air come and lodge in the branches thereof."

33 Jesus continued with another parable, saying, "The kingdom of heaven is like the yeast used to make bread which a woman took and mixed with three cups of flour making the whole mixture leavened."

34 Jesus spoke all these parables to the multitude of peoples, and didn't speak without using one in what he had to teach that day.

35 Also written of Moses by Asaph in his Psalm, a recorder during the reign of King Hezekiah of Jerusalem.

36 Then Jesus sent the multitude of peoples away and went into the house he was staying at. His disciples came up to him and asked, "Tell us what this parable of the weeds in the field meant."

37 He answered and said to them, "The person that is planting the good seed is the Son of man,

38 The field is the world, the good seed are the children of the kingdom, but the weeds are the children of the Devil,

39 The enemy that has planted them amongst the good seed, is the devil, the harvest is the end of this world the day this world ends for you when you die, and the reapers are the angels of the Lord in heaven.

40 As in the parable, the weeds or 'unrighteous' persons will be destroyed just as the weeds are burned in the fire, so shall it be to those found unworthy on the day they leave this world.

41 After I leave this world, I will send forth the angels, throughout heaven to gather out of his kingdom all those who are not worthy and those who does not belong amongst the holy.

42 And will cast them out into this realm of the devil, and there shall be much suffering for them for all eternity.

43 Then shall the righteous shine forth as the sun in the kingdom of their Father in heaven. Who ever is listening, may they hear this truth.

44 For the kingdom of heaven is like treasure that is buried in a field, that when a

person finds it, overjoyed hides it and sells all he has and then buys that field.

45 The Kingdom of Heaven is also like a merchant, seeking the finest pearls,

46 Who, when that merchant found a pearl of worth alot of money, selling for a low price, goes and sells all he has and buys that pearl.

47 The kingdom of heaven is also like a net that was cast into the sea, and gathers all kinds of creatures from the sea within it,

48 Which, when it was full, they brought it ashore, and sat down selecting what is good from the catch into their fishing vessels and throwing back all those creatures not worthy of eating.

49 So shall it be for each person at the end of this life for the angels will come forth and separate the wicked from the just,

50 And cast the wicked into the realm of the devil where there is much suffering for all eternity."

51 Then Jesus asked them, "Have you understood all these things?" They answered and said unto him, "Yes, Lord."

52 Jesus continued and said, "Therefore every apostle that is instructed in the knowledge of the kingdom of heaven is like the owner of a house who owns alot treasures, for you own the knowledge of the past and the present.

53 And it came to pass, that when Jesus finished all these parables, he departed from that city.

54 When he entered into his own country of Israel, he taught the peoples in the Jewish synagogue, and many of the peoples were so astonished that they exclaimed, "How does this man have so much wisdom, and how does he do these mighty works?"

55 Isn't this the son of Joseph the carpenter and isn't his mother's name Mary? Aren't his brothers James, Joses, Simon, and Judas?

56 And of his sisters, we also know who they are? How is it that we know this man and his simple family that he could be so wise and knowledgeable?"

57 At that moment they began to act offended by him. But Jesus said unto them, "A prophet is not without honor, except in his own country, and his own house."

58 Then he left without doing or saying anything more because of their lack of faith in him.

CHAPTER 14

1 About the same time, King Herod the fourth, heard of Jesus and his fame,

2 In fear, he told his servants, "This man has to be John the Baptist who has risen from the dead as he does many miracles that can't be explained."

3 For Herod the fourth had John the Baptist arrested, and kept him in shackles, locked up in a cell in his prison because his brother Phillip's wife, Herodias, despised him, for

4 Telling the King that it was unlawful to commit adultery with her, so she had him arrested for it,

5 The King would not put John the Baptist to death, fearing that if he did, it would create a rebellion amongst his followers, since they considered him a prophet.

6 But on the day of the King's birthday, they held a celebration and the daughter of Herodias danced before them, which pleased the king.

7 For it, the king promised with an oath that he would give her anything she so desired in his kingdom. All she needed to do was ask.

8 Being enticed by her mother to do so, Herodias' daughter said, "Give me the head of John the Baptist on a plater."

9 The king felt remorse for having made such an oath, but commanded some of his soldiers who were at the table eating with them to carry out the order of beheading John, bringing it on a plater to Herodias' daughter.

10 The soldiers got up and carried out the order they were given.

11 And John the Baptist's head was brought on a plater, and given to the daughter who presented it to her mother.

12 When the disciples of John heard of his execution, they came and asked for his body and his head, and was buried. Afterwards, the disciples of John went and informed Jesus of his death.

13 When Jesus heard of his cousin John's death, he was moved, and departed by ship into coasts of the land of Egypt and dwelt there in a desert place apart from many peoples, but when the peoples heard he was there, they found him and

began to follow him on foot, having come from out of their cities.

14 Jesus went forth, and saw a great multitude of peoples gathering and was moved with compassion toward them, and began to heal their sick.

15 That evening, his apostles came up to him, saying, "This is a desert place, and nobody has had anything to eat, why don't you send the peoples away to go into their villages so that they might buy themselves some food to eat."

16 But Jesus replied, "They don't need to leave, give them something to eat."

17 Looking at all the peoples there the apostles answered, "How can we feed so many when all we have is five loaves of bread and two fishes?"

18 Jesus said, "Bring them here to me."

19 And he commanded the multitude of peoples to sit down on the grass of an oasis they were at and took the five loaves, and two fishes, and looking up to heaven, blessed them, and began to divide the bread and the fishes into baskets, which he began to give to his apostles and the disciples around him to take to the crowd of peoples there.

20 As the evening went on, they all ate and everyone was full. Picking up the leftovers from the meal they all shared, they took up bread and fish that filled twelve baskets.

21 Of all the peoples that ate that evening, were about five thousand men, not including women and children.

22 Right afterwards, Jesus sent the multitude of peoples away, and went up into a mountain to pray by himself.

23 Coming down from the mountain, he told the apostles to board the ship so they could leave and go back to Israel.

24 As the ship was on the shore in the midst of the sea, it was real windy and tossed the ship about heavily upon the waves,

25 It was about 10 o'clock at night, as Jesus was seen walking upon the sea.

26 When the apostles saw him walking on the sea, it greatly bothered them and scared them and said, "Is it a spirit?"

27 But hearing this, Jesus immediately comforted them by saying, "Don't be scared,

it's just me, so be glad."

28 Peter not being able to see him in the night, said, "Lord, if it's you, help me to come up to you upon the water."

29 Jesus replied, "Don't be afraid, come." And when Peter stepped out of the ship and put his feet upon the sea, he walked upon it up to Jesus.

30 Peter, seeing that the wind was blowing very strong, was very scared and began to sink. In a cry of desperation he yelled out, "Lord, save me!"

31 And immediately Jesus stretched out his hand, and caught him before he sank, and said. "Why do you have such little faith in my abilities that you doubt in them?" Peter felt ashamed but glad that Jesus save him.

32 Taking hold of Peter's hand, they both walked upon the sea up to side of the ship and boarded it. By then the wind subsided and calmed down.

33 Once upon the ship, the other apostles and a few disciples began to worship Jesus, saying, "Now we know it is true, that you are the Son of the Lord in heaven."

34 Traveling through the night , the ship came upon the shores of the land of Gennesaret.

35 When the peoples found out that Jesus landed upon their shores, they sent out word amongst the peoples of their country and brought to him the persons afflicted with all kinds of illnesses and disease.

36 Some of the peoples came up to him asking him if they could touch the hem of his garment that they could be healed.

CHAPTER 15

1 Then came some scribes and Pharisees up to Jesus which were of Jerusalem, saying,

2 "Why do your apostles transgress the tradition of the elders of our religion by not washing their hands before they eat bread?"

3 Jesus answered and said to the scribes and Pharisees, "Why do you also transgress the commandment of Yahveh you believe in your tradition?

4 Didn't your God Yahveh state in your commandment to honor your father and mother, for the one who curses their father and mother, should be put to death.

5 But you change that by saying, Whoever says to their father or mother, it is a gift I am born by what ever you profit from me,

6 So you don't honor your father or your mother because you feel you are free men and don't have to honor them. Doesn't this make the commandment of your God Yahveh worthless within your tradition?

7 You hypocrites, well did your prophet Isaiah prophesied of you, when he wrote,

8 'These peoples draw themselves close to me with their mouths, and honor me with their lips, but their hearts are far from me.

9 In vain they worship me, teaching as doctrines, the commandments of men.'"

10 And he called the multitude of peoples to gather around him and said unto them, "Hear and understand what I say,

11 It is not that which goes into your mouths that defile you, but that which comes out of your mouths. 'This' is what defiles a person."

12 Then the apostles came up to him and said, "Did you know that you offended the scribes and Pharisees by what you just said?"

13 But he answered and said, "Every plant, which my heavenly Father has not planted, is not part of his harvest.

14 Leave them alone, they are blind leaders leading a following who is also blind. And if the blind, lead the blind, how can they save themselves from falling into the ditch the devil has prepared for them."

15 Then Peter asked him, "Tell us what you mean by this parable."

16 And Jesus disappointingly said, "Are you still not able to understand what I am teaching you?"

17 Don't you understand yet, that what ever you put in your mouth goes into the body, and is cast out of it the following day. It not what you eat that defile you,

18 But those things which you say are the things that come out of your mouth for they come out of your mind and your heart, and if you are of bad behaviors, attitudes or beliefs, it is these things that will ruin you.

19 For out of the mind and heart come evil thoughts, murders, adultery, fornication, thefts, liars, violence, wars and blasphemy against the Lord.

20 These are the things which defile a person, NOT eating food with unwashed hands."

21 Then Jesus and the apostles left for the coasts of Tyre and Sidon.

22 Arriving at their destination, a woman of Canaan ran up to them crying out in desperation exclaiming, "Have mercy on me, oh Lord, thou Son of David, my daughter is grievously possessed by a devil."

23 But he didn't answered her nor did he say a word. His apostles, pleading with him said, "Send her away, she already offended you by calling you a Son of David, and is crying for us to help her."

24 But he answered and said, "The reason I haven't answered her is not for what she called me but because I have come only for the lost persons of the house of Israel."

25 Then she came worshiping him, pleading, "Lord, help me."

26 But he answered and said, "It is not right for me to give that which belongs to the children of heaven to a person who doesn't even know who I am, for it is as though I cast it to the dogs."

27 And she said, "Is true, Lord, but even the dogs eat the crumbs which fall from their masters table."

28 Hearing this, Jesus replied, "Woman, your faith in me is greater than your knowledge of who I am, and it is that faith that has healed your daughter." And at

that instant, the devil who possessed her daughter was cast out.

29 And all of them left the coasts of Sidon and Tyre. Upon coming to the Sea of Galilee, Jesus went up into a mountain to pray and be alone with the Father in heaven. When he got there he sat down and prayed.

30 Descending from the mountain, great multitudes of peoples came up to him, many of which were lame, blind, dumb, maimed, and many others afflicted with illness or disease, many of which threw themselves down at Jesus's feet, and he and the apostles healed them all.

31 The multitude was amazed when they saw the dumb speak, the maimed healed, the lame walk, and the blind able to see, and glorified Amen.

32 Then Jesus called his apostles unto him and said, "My heart feels heavy for all the peoples here because they have been with us three days now without food or drink, and I can't send them away fasting as many of them will faint from the lack of nourishment."

33 So the apostles asked him, "Where are we going to get so much food out here in the wilderness, as to fill so many people?"

34 Jesus questioned, "How many loaves of bread do we have?" They said, "Seven, and a few little fishes."

35 So Jesus asked everyone there to sit down on the ground,

36 And he took the seven loaves and the fishes, and gave thanks unto the Father for them, and began to brake the loaves apart, handing the baskets to his apostles who started to pass them around amongst the crowd there. He did the same thing with the fish.

37 And as everyone ate, they ate until everyone was full and took up the leftovers from the meal, which filled seven baskets.

38 Of the multitude Jesus fed that day were a total of four thousand men, excluding the women and children.

39 He then sent the peoples home, then he and the apostles left to board the ship and sailed for the coasts of Magdala.

Note Verse 39 ;

Mark's book states parts of Dalmanutha, but Mark was a "disciple" who joined the faith "after" Jesus had already been crucified. Only the Apostle Matthew, from which this writing is taken from "mentions" the coasts of Magdala, of which is an apostle who was actually, "there."

CHAPTER 16

1 The Pharisees and Sadducees came, seducing Jesus into showing them a sign from heaven.

2 He answered and said to them, "When it's evening, you say, It will be fair weather , for the sky is red.

3 And in the morning, you say, It will be foul weather today, for the sky is red and cloudy. You hypocrites, how is it that you can discern the weather by how the sky appears, but can't discern the signs of the time?

4 A wicked and adulterous generation seeks to see a sign, and there will be no sign given to it, but the sign of the your prophet Jonah." Then Jesus walked away from them and he and the apostles boarded the ship and departed Magdala.

5 When out at sea, the apostles began to get hungry and remembered that they forgot to bring bread to eat on board.

6 Then Jesus said to them, "Beware, don't forget the doubt the Pharisees and Sadducees had in Magdala,

7 They reasoned amongst themselves by saying, This man is said to have fed thousands, so we will ask him for a sign to feed us as we have no bread,'

8 Which I was aware of and perceived from them, but why do you who have seen my abilities, doubt, by having such little faith by reasoning to yourselves you will go hungry because you brought no bread?

9 Don't you remember the five loaves of bread which fed five thousand people, and how many baskets of leftovers you took up?

10 How about the seven loaves which fed four thousand people. How many baskets did you take up then?

11 How is it that you don't understand what bothers me is not that you are concerned over not having brought bread, but the doubt in my abilities to provide it, which I don't understand coming from you for you know better and should be made aware of it. Don't you know it is the 'same' doctrines which the Pharisees and Sadducees live by in Magdala?"

12 Then they understood what it was that Jesus wanted them to understand, for it was not the bread which concerned him, but belief that the Lord is able to provide, which the doctrines of the Pharisees and Sadducees 'question.'

13 When Jesus and the apostles came upon the coasts of Caesarea Philippi, he asked his apostles, "Who do people say I am?"

14 They answered, "Some say you are John the Baptist, some say you are Elijah, and yet others say you are Jeremiah, or one of their Hebrew prophets."

15 He questioned them and said, "Who do you say I am?"

16 And the apostle Simon Peter replied, "You are the Osiris on earth, the Son of the living Father in heaven."

17 Jesus said to him, "Blessed are you, Simon Barjona, for it wasn't a person of flesh and blood that revealed this to you, for it is a revelation given to you by my Father in heaven.

18 And I also say to you, you are my apostle Peter, and upon your firm faith will I build within you my temple, for you are as a rock that the gates of hell will not prevail against you.

19 I will give to you the wisdoms of the kingdom of heaven, and what ever I teach you to restrict on earth are those behaviors not found in heaven, and what ever I teach you to allow on earth, are those behaviors allowed in heaven."

20 Then he ordered his apostles not to tell anyone that he was Jesus, Osiris on earth , to offer an example to all humanity that there is eternal life.

21 From that time forward, Jesus began to show his apostles how he must go to Jerusalem and suffer alot of persecution because of the Jewish elders, chief priests and scribes, eventually, being arrested and killed by their accusations of him, but he would be resurrected by the Father in heaven three days later.

22 Then Peter shook him and like a lost child exclaimed, "Don't even say such things Lord, for nothing like that is going to happen to you."

23 But he turned, and said to Peter, "Get thee behind me, Satan, you are an offence to me, for you don't savor the things that are of Amen, but those that be of the flesh."

24 Then Jesus said to the apostles, "If anyone wants to be of my purpose, let them deny their desires in this life and do as I do and practice all I have taught and follow me in example.

25 For who ever will save their life for the evils of this world will lose it, but whoever loses their life in my purpose of saving humanity will find it.

26 For what will it profit a person, if they gain the whole world, but lose their soul in the process, for there isn't anything in this world that a person can give in exchange or 'buy' their own soul.

27 For the Son of the Lord will come in the glory of his Father with his angels, and then he will reward every person according to their works.

28 Amen-Ra says to tell you, There will be some standing here, which will not taste of death until they see the Son of Amen coming in his kingdom.

Note Verse 28

One of the most commonly used phases Jesus (Yeshua) used that was written within the Books of the Apostles was with this word " Verily. " There are other phrases he used which were recorded in the gospel writings but none which tell a conclusive narrative to Jesus having been a "scholar" of the Egyptian faith. Verily, is a WORD that that goes back thousands of years to a FAITH that RECORDS this " phase " within their sacred papyri. Egypt. Only " one " of many "familiarities" within the words Jesus " used " which tells a " Theban Disciple " who reads any Christian bible that Jesus READ the ancient sacred books of the Egyptian faith. Much of what Jesus "taught" is "written" not in Judaism, but in the ancient faith books of "EGYPT." Just in the way Jesus "chastised" the Jews of his day, shows that he was NOT of the Jewish FAITH. Jesus, was of the order of the Egyptian Therapeut Monks * (Essenes) *, which included Jewish converts who "saw" that something was wrong in the views Jews held in a "God of Wrath," yet he was "good?" The Essenes had a commune at Qumran, around the Dead Sea. "Modern" Judaism, as well as those of the day of Jesus, did not/do not practice the faith as given to the Hebrew of ancient times, and Jesus tried to "explain" this one FACT to the Pharisees, Sadducees as well as many Jews of his day. For it, Jewish leaders had him put to death, not in the "glory" of Judeo-Christian belief, but "murdered" for the truth as a Theban, to PROVE he WAS the Son of the Lord in heaven which no one can KILL. Proving the ancient Egyptian faith in the RESURRECTION, or LIFE AFTER DEATH.

(References of a few examples given on the next page which prove that Jesus was not of the Jewish faith are written within many of the holy books of the faith in the Lord of Creation in Egyptian beliefs. Within those books, for those who read these truths, clarity will come within all Jesus taught)

> Holy Sacraments of the Priest Ani, who served Ramses II and wrote many records dating back to when he lived around 1240 b.c., within the ancient Book of the Dead. (British Museum Archive)

> Egyptian Priest, Nu, sheets, 6, 13. (British Museum Archive)

> Egyptian Priest, Auf-ankh in the Turin papyri. (Turin, Italy)

> Egyptian Priest, Nebseni, sheet 21. (British Museum Archive)

CHAPTER 17

1 Six days after they had returned from Caesarea Philippi, Jesus took Peter, with him to go up into a high mountain.

2 Having climbed to the top, Jesus looked up to the sky and his face and his clothes began to glow and shine as an exceedingly bright light much like the sun, as Peter watched while Jesus was transformed.   (*Note* in Index)

3 Then Peter said to Jesus, "Lord, it is good for us to be here, but if you will allow me,

4 I will make us a tabernacle where we can pray and meditate upon the Father,"

5 But while he was talking a bright cloud overshadowed them, and behold, a voice out of the cloud, which said, "This is my beloved Son, in whom I am well pleased, listen to all he has to teach."

6 When Peter heard Amen speak to them, he fell upon his knees and bowed his face to the ground, for he became very frightened.

7 Jesus came up to him and touched him on the shoulder and said, "Get up, my son don't be afraid."

8 When Peter rose up from the ground, he lifted up his eyes to the sky but the cloud was gone and all he could see was Jesus.

9 As they came down from the mountain, Jesus told Peter, "Don't tell the vision to anyone, until after I suffer death and have risen from the dead."

10 Then Peter asked him a question and said, "Why did Isaiah write that Elijah must come first before you?"

11 Jesus answered, "Isaiah, the Hebrew prophet was a wise man, but his words have been misperceived of Elijah and me, for Elijah had to come first and prepare the way."

12 But I say to you, "Elijah has already come, and the peoples didn't even know who he was, killing him as evil men do, and just as they killed him, they will also kill me."

13 Then Peter understood that he was telling him of John the Baptist, and what was

to be in the days to come.

14 When they returned, there were many peoples, and a certain man came up to them kneeling down in front of Jesus saying,

15 "Lord, have mercy on my son, for he is mentally afflicted with an illness that makes him disoriented many times to where he falls into things for no reason.

16 And I brought him to your apostles but they couldn't cure him."

17 Then Jesus looked upon the rest of his apostles and answered, "Oh faithless and perverse generation, how long must I be with you and how long will I put up with doubt? Sir, bring your son to me."

18 And Jesus rebuked the illness within the boy, and it left him. In that moment was the child cured.

19 Then the apostles took Jesus aside and asked, "Why couldn't any of us cure the young child?

20 Jesus sternly looked at them and said, "It is because of your lack of confidence in your abilities that gives you unbelief in them, for Amen-Ra says to tell you, If you had the faith as small as a mustard seed, you would have enough faith and capability to say to this mountain remove yourself from this place and go yonder, and it would remove itself, for nothing would be impossible to you.

21 How is it that people who lack confidence in themselves are always so wrapped up in prayer and fasting and accomplish nothing else. "Then Jesus walked away from them with Peter by his side.

22 During their stay in Galilee, one day Jesus said to the apostles, "I will be betrayed by one of you and turned over to men,

23 Who will kill me, but on the third day after I am put to death I will rise from the dead. "And they looked at each other feeling exceeding sorry, for they didn't know who it was that would betray him.

24 Leaving Galilee, they went to Capernaum where tax collectors came up to Peter and asked, "Does your master pay taxes?"

25 He said, "Yes." And when they arrived at the house they were to stay in, Yezua took Peter aside and said, "What were you thinking of by lying Simon? Which

persons do the kings of the earth take gifts or money from? Their children or strangers?"

26 Peter replied, "Of strangers." Then Jesus said, "So their children don't have to pay taxes, and live for free, and we are strangers to them, right?

27 Before we offend them by finding out you were lying, go get a fishing pole, go up to the sea and cast the hook into the sea and the fish which you will catch, open up it's mouth and you will find a coin. Take that money and give it to the tax collectors for it will be enough and tell them it's from all of us.

Note Verse 3

This verse is left out of Matthew's accounts, as "none" of the apostles who are said to have gone up into the mountain with Jesus even made an accounting of this incident ever having taken place which seems odd considering "3" apostles are said to have gone with Jesus by Matthew, Mark and Luke and none of them wrote of such a happening ever having taken place. It is a bad attempt at trying to "link" Jesus to Judaism by proclaiming Moses and Elijah were at this event. It is also a bad attempt to include James and John, as authoritative figures selected out of the rest of the apostles along with Peter by Jesus, to be "present" when Jesus speaks with the Lord in heaven, and as truth goes James and John, were not on good terms with Jesus or the rest of the apostles when it came to humility. In this story they are "left out."

CHAPTER 18

1 At about the same time came the apostles up to Jesus, saying, "Who is the greatest in the kingdom of heaven?"

2 Jesus called a little child to come to him, and set him in the midst of them,

3 And said, "Amen-Ra says to tell you, unless you are converted and become as little children in nature, you will not enter into the kingdom of heaven.

4 Whoever humbles themselves to be as this little child, is greatest in the kingdom of heaven,

5 And who ever receives such a person in my name, is as though they receive me.

6 But whoever offends one of my little children which believes in me, would be better off if they hung a heavy stone around their neck and threw themselves into the depths of the sea.

7 I feel sorry for those in this world who live by bad behaviors, though there will always be these kinds of peoples, but it will be even worse for the persons who encourage or teach others to live by them.

8 If there is a behavior or attitude that is wrong in your life, change it by cutting it out of your lifestyle though it may hurt, for it is better that you rid yourself of these vices than to lose your reward in the afterlife.

9 If that one of your bad habits is caused by those evil things you see which tempt you into bad behaviors, of which are many, look the other way and cut those things out of your life for good or lose your reward in the afterlife.

10 Be alert in your attitudes. Don't despise or envy another person on earth or in faith, for I say to you, the angels in heaven know how you feel in secret and are those beings which inform the Father in heaven.

11 For I have come to save those persons who are lost in the ways of this world, don't know the ways of heaven or assume they know what they are.

12 Tell me what you think of this story. A man has a hundred sheep, and one of them goes astray. Doesn't he leave the ninety-nine alone to go search for the lost one that strayed away, even if he has to go up into the mountains?

13 Amen-Ra says to tell you, when he finds it, doesn't he rejoice alot more for that one sheep, than the other ninety-nine which did not get lost?

14 As such, it isn't the will of your Father in heaven that anyone perish, especially his children, but he is also concerned for those who are lost, and just like that lost sheep, he continually searches to find those lost to his ways hoping they find them.

15 Amongst the faithful, if a person has transgressed another, let the offended go up to the transgressor to ask for a discussion amongst themselves in secret, If accepted, both sides may gain a friend.

16 But if the transgressor refuses the discussion, next time take one or two other persons as a witness of your intentions. Again, ask for a discussion.

17 If the transgressor still refuses, take the matter up of having made good intentions to settle an offense with the congregation of the faithful and allow one from amongst them to ask the transgressor in front of the congregation for that discussion in secret. If the transgressor still refuses to settle their offense, refuse their company as part of the faithful.

18 Amen-Ra says to tell you, What ever I teach you to bind on earth is because it is not allowed in heaven, and what ever I teach you is allowed on earth, is because it is allowed in heaven.

19 Where two of you gather together and agree on earth upon asking for and touch anything worthy of your calling, it will be done for them by my Father in heaven.

20 Where two or three are gathered together in my name, there am I in the midst of them.

21 Then Peter asked him, "Lord, what is the limit on how often anyone can transgress against us, and we are bound to forgive them?"

22 Jesus replied, "I said, until seventy times seven, but the world is evil and those of the devil rely on forgiveness so they do not have to change. And if a person expects to be forgiven what lesson will they learn of consequence? Change does not come by escaping our behaviors, it comes by paying the prices for the bad ones, so we don't constantly repeat them.   (*Note* @ end of Chapter)

23 I compare the kingdom of heaven is like a certain king, who was looking over his ledger on what his servants owed him.

24 When he began to look at the ledger he had one of the servants brought before him who owed him ten thousand talents.

25 Telling him that he has never tried to repay him, his lord commanded that he, his wife, his children, and all that he had, be sold to repay his debt.

26 Immensely scared, the servant fell down before him, began to worship him, saying, 'Lord, have patience with me, and I will repay you all I owe.'

27 The lord of that servant felt sorry for him and was moved with compassion, so much so, that he let him go and forgave his debt.

28 But that same servant went out and found one of his fellow servants who owed him a hundred pence and grabbed him by the throat, saying, 'Pay me what you owe me, now!'

29 The fellow servant fell down at his feet, and pleaded with him saying, 'Have patience with me. I don't have the money now, but I will pay you.'

30 But the servant had no compassion upon his fellow servant and had him put in prison until he repayed him his debt.

31 When the other servants of the lord saw what this one servant did to the other one, they went and told their lord what he did.

32 Then the lord summoned the servant whose debt he had forgiven and when he came before him said, 'How could you be so wicked to your fellow servant? You stood before me and pleaded with me over the money you owed me and out of compassion I forgave you that debt.

33 Don't you think you should have shown that same compassion to your fellow servant just as I had pity on you?'

34 His lord was very angry, and for his lack of compassion and his behaviors, he delivered him to tormentors, who put him to work until he paid back all the ten thousand talents he owed the his lord.

35 So will it be given by the Father in heaven to those who lack compassion one to another. To forgive is compassionate when the transgressor is truly sorry for an

offense.

36 To forgive a transgressor who uses it to further transgress will not change.

37 Of such, Satan has need to torment, who may one day grow tired of their own behaviors and mature.

38 Then may they become an instrument of the Father in heaven in a faith which is as a rock, firm and in the wisdom of the Lord, Amen in heaven.

Note Verse 22

    This verse was written by Amen John I, for Jesus instructed what is written in relation to all that has happened over the course of the last 20 centuries. Behavior has CONSEQUENCE, and no longer will forgiveness be an escape for the bad ones perpetrated upon humanity, by religions or any others. This WORD is from the HOLY in heaven, and a RETURN to the NEW KINGDOM on earth, as it WAS within the Egyptian Dynasty when Tut Ahmose I in 1586 b.c., was told by the Lord to "fight" evil with the same fire as the enemy which persecuted it and took back the land which the Lord in heaven gave to his faithful. Not mentioned in the Torah, but these " invaders " overthrown were Hebrew ancestors, and "then" became "slaves" to Egypt. (Written within the chronologies of Egypt on papyri)

Verses 35-38

Written of Amen John I

CHAPTER 19

1 Later, after Jesus finished these sayings, he and the twelve apostles departed from Galilee, and traveled along the coasts of the Mediterranean sea until they reached the border of Judah that lay beyond the river Jordan.

2 By then, great multitudes of peoples were following them, and they stopped for awhile so Jesus could heal some of them there.

3 The Pharisees also happened to be amongst the crowd and came up to him, hoping to tempt Jesus said, "Is it lawful for a man to put away his wife for every cause?

4 And Jesus answered, "Haven't you read, that the Lord who made them in the beginning made them male and female, and

5 For this cause shall a man leave father and mother, and shall cleave to his wife, and they both shall be of one flesh?

6 Wherefore they are no longer two persons of the flesh but one. What therefore the Lord has joined together, let not man put asunder."

7 The Pharisees asked again, "Why did Moses then command the men that if they could not get along with their wives to give her a writing of divorcement, and put her away?"

8 Jesus replied, "Moses said that to them because out of the hardness of your hearts you are going to put your wives away whether or not you have just cause, but from the beginning it wasn't that way.

9 I am telling you that whoever gets rid of his wife except it be for fornication and marries another, commits adultery, and who ever marries his wife, is also guilty of committing adultery, including that wife that is put away."

10 Hearing this, the apostles said to him, "If that's the case then, would it not be better for people not to get married?"

11 Jesus said, "This message isn't for all persons, except for those men and women who make it a habit of leaving their spouses so they can fulfill their sexual desires with someone else, which is the same as adultery for they use divorce as a way to legally be with someone else, but is not legal within the laws of the Lord in

heaven.

12 For there are some people born sterile, some have medical procedures done to make themselves sterile and then there are those who make themselves sterile for the sake of the kingdom of heaven so they will not suffer sexual desires as a temptation on earth. Let the one who knows what I mean receive what I just said." (*Note* in Index)

13 Then some people brought up to him their children so that Jesus could touch and pray for them, but the apostles tried to turn them away.

14 But Jesus said, "Don't turn them away, let them come unto me, for of their nature are the holy in heaven.

15 And he prayed as he laid his hands upon them, then left.

16 As he did, a person abruptly stopped him and said, "Good Master, what good thing can I do, that I may have eternal life?"

17 And he said unto him, "Why do you call me good? There is nobody good but Amen in heaven, and if you want a better life, adhere to your commandments.

18 The person asked, "Which ones?" And Jesus answered, "Do not murder, Do not commit adultery, Don't steal, Don't bear false witness against your neighbor,

19 Honor your father and mother and Love your neighbor like you love yourself."

20 The young man said, "But I've done all those things ever since I was a boy, do I lack anything else?"

21 Then Jesus answered, "Only one thing if you wish to be perfect. Go and sell everything you own, give to the poor, and you will gain treasure in heaven, then come and follow me."

22 But when the young man heard that, he went away very depressed because he owned alot of great possessions.

23 Jesus turned to his apostles and said, "Amen-Ra says to tell you, That a rich person will have a hard time entering the kingdom of heaven.

24 It is much easier for a camel to go through the eye of a needle, than for a rich person to enter into the kingdom of Amen."

25 When his apostles heard this, they were exceedingly puzzled and amongst them-

selves wondered if this be so then who can be saved?

26 But Jesus overheard them and said, "Within the powers of the flesh this is impossible, but with those of Amen in heaven, all things are possible."

27 Then Peter asked, "We have all given up everything we owned to follow you, haven't we, so what will we gain for it?"

28 And Jesus said unto them, "Amen-Ra says to tell you, That you who have followed me in this generation will sit upon twelve thrones along side me on my throne in glory, helping me to judge all those upon earth.

29 And every one that has forsaken houses, family, friends or lands, for my name's sake, will gain it all back a hundredfold and will inherit everlasting life.

30 But of the many who will enter heaven, the greatest ones will be of the least important while the least will be the most important.

Note Verse 11 and 12

Verse 11, clearly states that the Hebrew law Moses gave, is not the same as the law of Lord regarding divorce, for people have found ways to abuse this law, and pegged it as being just in the eyes of the Lord. It is why Jesus has made it clear that divorcing someone simply for the reason of marrying someone else whom we find more desirable than another is still adultery. I have had many who question why the things Jesus said about divorce did not include physical abuse or incompatibility. On the subject of abuse, the Lord is clear. We should never subject ourselves to living a life where we jeopardize the serenity of the spirit. This also pretty much covers incompatibility. Not all marriages whine up being between two people who later find out they have nothing in common. Though religion sees divorce as undesirable and a part that people should work out once married, much of this advice comes from those ignorant to what comprises a relationship between two opposing forces under one roof. Marriage "works," only when TWO people are willing to work at it. Much of the failures in marriage come when one of the partners is not willing to humble themselves to the other and the Lord. A happy marriage is one where "both" parties are in harmony with the Lord and each other.

Verse "12" clarifies that there are "persons," born, medically altered or choose to exclude sex from their lives for reason pertaining to temptations of the flesh which in turn give them the strenght to resist evil and do the will of the Lord in heaven. In this verse Jesus is pretty much explaining "his" choice, and that of his Apostles.

CHAPTER 20

1 Another example of what the kingdom of heaven is like, is an owner of a house who went out early one morning to hire laborers to work in his vineyard.

2 When he found some, they agreed upon working for a penny a day, whereupon he sent the laborers out into the vineyard to work.

3 The owner then went out again 3 hours later, or about 9 o'clock in the morning and saw some more persons standing idle in the marketplace,

4 He asked them, if they needed work, he needed more laborers for his vineyard and would pay what is right, and give it to them. They accepted and went to work in his vineyard.

5 Again, around noon and again, around 3 o'clock in the afternoon, he hired more laborers to work in the vineyard.

6 At 5 o'clock that same afternoon he went out and found other persons standing around idle, asked them, 'Why have been standing around idle all day?'

7 They told, 'Because nobody has hired us.' So the owner said to them, 'Go out into my vineyard and if you work I will pay you what is right for it.'

8 That evening, the lord of the vineyard said to his foreman, 'Call the laborers in, and pay them for the day, beginning with the last ones I hired up to the first which I put to work early this morning.'

9 When the laborers he hired at 5 o'clock came to collect their wages for the day, they each received a penny, as did those laborers he hired at noon and 3 o'clock.

10 But when those he hired at 6 o'clock in the morning came to collect their wages, they felt they deserved to be paid more as they worked longer.

11 But when they received their wages, it was also a penny, getting upset with the owner of the vineyard.

12 Saying, 'These last laborers you hired only worked one hour, while we have worked since 6 o'clock this morning bearing the load of all the work in the heat of the day, and you paid them the same as us?'

13 He answered them and said, 'Friends, I didn't do you wrong. Didn't you agree this

morning to work for the day for a penny?

14 Take your wages and go. I choose to pay these last ones I hired the same as I paid you.

15 It's not against the law for me to do what I want with my own money and just because you think it unfair, doesn't affect my kindness.'

16 So will it be in heaven, for the last will receive the same as the first, and the first will receive the same as the last, for many will be called, but few will be chosen."

17 As Jesus and the apostles left Judah on their way to Jerusalem, he took the twelve apostles aside and said,

18 "Behold, we are on our way to Jerusalem where I will be betray unto the Jewish scribes and chief priests there and they will condemn me to be put to death,

19 And they will deliver me up unto the Gentiles to be mocked by them, made fun of, tortured and they will crucify me, but on the third day after I am put to death, I will be resurrected to be amongst you again."

20 Then came the mother of Zebedee's children, James and John, up to him, worshiping and desiring a certain thing from him.

21 And Jesus asked her, "What is it that you want from me?" And she said, "Grant that in the afterlife that my two sons may sit, one on your right hand and the other on the left, in your kingdom."

22 Jesus answered her and her sons, and said, "You don't know this thing you are asking me to do. Are you able to bear the burdens I have to bear, and to be baptized with the baptism that I am baptized with? "And they said, "Yes, we are able."

23 Jesus told them, "You will indeed bear the same burdens and you will be baptized with the same baptism that I am baptized with, but for one of you to sit on my right hand, while the other sits on my left, is not mine to give, for those places will be given to whom it has been prepared for by my Father in heaven."

24 When the other ten apostles heard the question James and John's mother asked Jesus her sons had put her up to, they were moved with indignation against the two brothers.

25 But Jesus called those ten apostles over to him and said, "You know that the apostles James and John are egotistical and allow the princes of the Gentiles to hold dominion over them, as well as others who are great in the world manipulate their faith.

26 But it won't be that way with the rest of you, and who ever choose to be great amongst you, let him be your priest,

27 And who ever is a doer amongst you, let him be your servant in faith,

28 Just as I have not come to be preached at, but to preach, I also came to die if need be for this purpose I am carrying out.

29 And as they departed, a great multitude of peoples followed them.

30 Along the way, two blind men were sitting along the path and when they heard that Jesus was passing by, cried out, saying, "Have mercy upon us, Oh Lord, thou Son of Amen."

31 And many from amongst the multitude got angry at them, because they should have held their tongue, but they cried out even louder, saying, "Have mercy on us, Oh Lord, thou Son of Amen!"

32 At that point, Jesus stood still, and called out to them and said, "What is it you want of me to do for your sake?

33 They say unto him, "Lord, just simply that our eyes be healed."

34 Jesus having compassion for them, touched their eyes, and immediately their eyes received sight, and both of them, followed him.

CHAPTER 21

1 When Jesus and the apostles were near Jerusalem at Bethphage upon the mount of Olives, Jesus sent two of the apostles to find an ass that he may ride upon into the city of Jerusalem, as it was close to the passover.

2 He said to the apostles, "Go into the village and there you will find an ass and a colt with her. Bring them to me.

3 If the owner shows up, tell him the Lord has need of them, and right away he will let you use them. (*Note* in Index)

4 This occurred just as the Hebrew prophet Haggai in the 6th century b.c. Wrote, stating,

5 "Rejoice greatly, O daughter of Zion; shout, O daughter of Jerusalem: behold, thy King cometh unto thee, he is just, and having salvation, lowly, and riding upon an ass, and upon a colt the foal of an ass."

6 And the two apostles went, and did as Jesus commanded them.

7 So the apostles went out and brought the ass, and the colt to him, and put some of their clothes upon one, and set Jesus thereon.

8 Alot of people from the great multitude who gathered round began to throw some of their garments along the path to Jerusalem while others cut down branches from the trees to smooth out the road in the way.

9 Many of the peoples up ahead and which followed cried out, "Hosanna to the Son of Amen, Blessed is he who comes in the name of the Lord, Hosanna in the highest."

10 As Jesus came near unto Jerusalem, most of the inhabitants of the city were wondering who he was and said, "Who is this?"

11 Many from the peoples who gathered exclaimed, "This is Jesus, the prophet of Nazareth in Galilee.

12 And Jesus went into that which they called the temple of Yahveh and began to throw out all those who were selling and buying things there in the temple, and threw over the tables of the moneychangers and the seats of those who were there

selling doves, oxen and sheep,

13 And said unto them, "It is written by your prophet Isaiah, My house shall be called the house of prayer," but all of you here, have made it a den of thieves.

14 After, the blind and the lame came to him in the temple, and he healed them.

15 When the chief priests and scribes saw the wonderful things that he did, and saw the children crying in the temple saying to Jesus, "Hosanna to the Son of Amen," the priests and scribes were very displeased,

16 And said to Jesus, "Are you listening to what they are calling you?" And Yezua answered, "Yes. Haven't you read in your book of Psalms, "Out of the mouth of babes and sucklings hast thou ordained strength because of thine enemies, that thou mightiest still the enemy and the avenger. When I consider thy heavens, the work of thy fingers, the moon and the stars, which thou hast ordained?"
(*Note* in Index)

17 Then the Jews asked Jesus, "What sign are you going to show us, seeing that you can do all these things?"

18 Jesus answered them and said, "Destroy this temple, and in three days I will raise it up."

19 Replied the Jews, "Forty-six years it took to build this temple, and you say you can build it in three days?"

20 But Jesus was speaking of the temple of his body.

21 It was later when Jesus rose from the dead that his disciples all remembered what he had said on this day,

22 When he was here in Jerusalem at the passover on the feast day and even more readily, believed in his name.

23 Jesus did not commit himself unto the Jews, because he knew how all persons are,

24 He also didn't need the testimony of anyone, for he knew what was in every person.

25 There was a man of the Pharisees, named Nicodemus, a ruler of the Jews,

26 Who came unto Jesus one night, and said, "Rabbi, we know that you are a teacher

come to us from the Lord, for no one can do these miracles that you do, unless Amen is in you."

27 Jesus replied, "Amen-Ra says to tell you, verily, Except a person be born again, they cannot see the kingdom of the Lord."

28 To which Nicodemus said, "How can a person be born when they are old?, can they enter a second time into their mother's womb, and be born?"

29 Jesus answered, "Amen-Ra says to tell you, verily, Except a person be born of water and of the Spirit, they cannot enter into the kingdom of Amen.

30 That which is born of the flesh is flesh, and that which is born of the Spirit is spirit.

31 Marvel not that I said unto you, You must be born again.

32 The wind blows where it wishes and you hear the sound of it when it does, but you can't tell from which direction it will come or from which direction it will go, so is everyone that is born of the Spirit."

33 Nicodemus questioned, "How can these things be?"

34 And Jesus answered, "Aren't you a master of Israel, and don't even know these things?"

35 Amen-Ra says to tell you, verily, We speak that you may know, and testify that which we have seen, and yet you can not receive our witness?

36 If I had taught you earthly things, and you don't believe, how will you believe, if I tell you of heavenly things?

INDEX*CHAPTER 21

Note Verses 1-7

Are questionable as to an event that "actually" took place. After the trip to Judah from Galilee and then up to Jerusalem, Jesus may have been tired and requested two of the apostles go find him a horse or an ass to ride the rest of the way and a "link" here made to the prophesy of Haggai in the 6th century b.c. "Questionable," because Haggai's references of the "King" calls him a bastard, NOT a Son of the Lord. One of the "psychological" points within all Jesus did while on earth was to "fulfill" what was written by the ancient Hebrew prophets "mainly" to convince them that the Jewish faith was NOT up to the standards of their own prophets nor the most holy one . Haggai's reference to the coming of Jesus was right when he called him a "bastard," (Ha 9:6) as the Jewish peoples thought of him as such, and to this day still is thought of in this manner by Christians and Jews. The "Son of David" statement made throughout translation's reflect upon this word bastard. Within Haggai's book is the reflection of a physical not "spiritual" King within his prophesy, who is sent to take control of unrighteousness and punish the enemies of Jerusalem for the God of their faith.

Understandable, since alot of the Jewish prophets consistently reflect upon a God of Wrath that is to destroy their enemies in the end, "psychologically" the obsession of cultures subject to oppression. Haggai writes his prophesy right after the Hebrew peoples release from their Babylonian captivity. (Ha 2:7-3:4)

There is one fact about the prophet Haggai not many address. When he made his prophesies he "included" a part of his visions that includes the Lord telling him that the doctrines of Hebrew faith are ones that have been "stolen" and "false," as I myself have stated. Herewith are those words written by the Hebrew prophet.

105

Haggai 5:1-4 ;

"Then I turned, and lifted up my eyes and looked, and behold I saw a flying roll. And the Lord said to me, "What do you see?" I said, "I see a flying roll, the length of which is twenty cubits, with a width of ten cubits." Then the Lord said to me, "This is the (false doctrines) curse that go forth over the face of the whole earth, for every one that (has doctored my holy words) steals will be cut off (on earth) as on this side according to it, and everyone that swears (by these doctrines,) will be cut off (in heaven) on that side according to it. I will bring (these doctrines) it forth, said the LORD of hosts, and it will enter into the house of the thief (thieves), and into the house of him (those) that swear falsely by my name, and it will remain in the midst of his (their) house, and will consume it with the timber (wood) thereof and the stones thereof."

It is the main reason for this book. To RETURN the doctrines to those given by the Lord in heaven as they WERE in the BEGINNING, "not" a modification, of those that have been doctored up by various cultures. If there was a Prophet of the past that knew the TRUTH, it was HAGGAI, though Hebrew, the Lord in heaven does not "select" prophets by race or prejudice as religion does. One of the most important facts that Haggai was probably aware of was "of" these false doctrines which were being written and being passed off as being "truth." During the 26th Dynasty of Egypt the Persians not only invaded Israel but they also invaded Egypt. It was during this Dynasty in Egypt that some very important "historical facts" came to light. The NAME of a God of "pre-dynasty" inhabitants of the Nile Valley. The name was "Yahweh." Could be theoretical but my "theorem" of "how" the Hebrews began to call their God Yahveh, comes from the period Persians were invading and making slaves out peoples including those of Israel "and" Egypt. HAGGAI, "knew" that their "holy words" were not "AUTHENTIC" and that alot of them were based on hearsay and assumptions. And as for God? Probably came out of the mouth of an Egyptian slave to Babylon during the same time Hebrews were held in captivity. During the 6th century b.c., much of the middle east suffered at the hands of Persian invaders and much of Egyptian hieroglyphics were unknown, but Flinders Petrie, who discovered these artifacts, and Dr. Murray, who wrote a book on his and her discoveries, also drew the same conclusions, that much of Judaism is written upon facts of "memory" and "assumptions" AFTER the babylonian captivity, and substantiates "why," many of the books are without many names, dates, or connected to actual historical events. Haggai, who lived during the second year of Darius the firsts' reign, was aware of the "deceit" made within what they call "HOLY."

Note Verse 16

"Proper wording" inserted here, as what was written in the King James version was not an accurate recollection written of that which is written in Psalms 8:2. "NO" account in any of hebrew scriptures "say" the lines written here in Matthew of the King James Version;

"Out of the mouth of babes and sucklings thou hast perfected praise?"

CHAPTER 22

1 No one has ascended up to heaven, but they that came down from heaven, even the Son of the Lord, which is in heaven.

2 As Moses lifted up the serpent in the wilderness, even so must the Son of the Lord be lifted up,

3 That whoever believes in him should not perish, but have eternal life.

4 For the Lord so loved the world, that he gave his only begotten Son, that whoever believes in him should not perish, but have everlasting life.

5 For the Lord sent not his Son into the world to condemn the world, but that the world through him might be saved.

6 For they that believe in him is not condemned, but the one who doesn't believe, is condemned already because they have not believed in the name of the only begotten Son of the Lord.

7 And this is the condemnation, that light is come into the world, and people loved darkness rather than light, because their deeds were evil.

8 For everyone that does evil, hates the light, nor do they come to the light, for fear their deeds will be exposed.

9 But the ones who do live in truth, come unto the light, for they are not ashamed of their deeds, for they aren't afraid of being exposed for who they are. The beloved of the Lord in heaven."

10 Jesus then left Jerusalem and went to Bethany, and lodged there.

11 Now in the morning as he went into the city, he was hungry.

12 Along the way he saw a fig tree and went up to it and found no fruit growing upon it, only leaves. Seeing the condition of the tree he said, "Let no fruit grow upon you forever," and the tree dried up.   (*Note* in Index)

13 When the disciples saw it, they were surprised and said, "That tree dried up real fast!"

14 Jesus answered and said, "Amen-Ra says to tell you, If you have faith and don't doubt, you will not be capable of this which was done to the fig tree, but will also

be capable of saying to a mountain, Remove yourself, and throw yourself into the sea, and it will happen.

15 And in all things, whatever you ask in prayer, believing, you will also receive." In the city he ate.

16 As Jesus continued walking, he went into the temple and began to teach. The chief priests and elders of the people came up to him, and said, "By what authority do you do these things?, and who gave you this authority?"

17 Jesus answered, "I also want to ask you one thing, which if you will tell me, I then, will answer your question on what authority I do these things.

18 On the baptism of John, from where did it come from? Heaven, or of men?" And they reasoned amongst themselves. If we say, from heaven, he will say to us, Why don't we believe in John the Baptist.

19 But if we say, of men, we are afraid of his disciples, for many revere John as having been a prophet.

20 So they answered Jesus and said, " We cannot tell." Jesus said unto them, " Neither will I tell you by what authority I do these things.

21 Listen and tell me what do you think of what I say here? A certain man had two sons. He came up to the first one and said, 'Son, go work today in my vineyard.'

22 The son answered his father and said, 'I will not,' but afterwards, repented, and did as the father had asked.

23 Then the father went up to the second son and said, 'Do likewise, and go work in the vineyard.' The son answered and said, 'I'll go, sir,' but didn't go.

24 Which one of them, did the will of his father?" The priests and elders said, "The first." Then Jesus said, "Amen-Ra says to tell you, That the publicans and the harlots go into the kingdom of Amen before you.

25 For John came to you in the way of righteousness, and you wouldn't believe in what he had to say, but the publicans and the harlots believed him. You even though you heard and saw his message, didn't even make the efforts to repent afterwards, so you too, might believe in him.

26 Hear this other parable, There was a certain owner of a house that planted a

vineyard, hedged it round about and dug a wine press in it, and also built a tower and left it in the hands of caretakers and went into a far country,

27 When the time of the fruit drew near, he sent his servants to the caretakers that they might receive the fruits of it.

28 But the caretakers took his servants, beat one, killed another, and stoned yet another.

29 Again, the owner, sent some more servants, more than he did the first time, and the caretakers did the same things to them.

30 Last of all, he sent unto them his son saying, 'They will reverence my son.'

31 But when the caretakers saw the owners son, they said amongst themselves, ' This is the heir. Come, let's kill him, and seize his inheritance.'

32 When they caught him, they cast him out of the vineyard, and slew him.

33 When the lord, owner of the vineyard returned, what do you think he did with those caretakers?"

34 The priests and elders replied, "He will miserably destroy those wicked men, and will let out his vineyard to some other caretakers, who will render him the fruits in their seasons."

35 Then Jesus said, "Did you ever read in the scriptures, the stone which the builders rejected, the same has become the head of the corner, this is the Lord's doing, and it is marvelous in our eyes?

36 Therefore do I say to you, The kingdom of the Lord shall be taken from you, and will be given to a nation bringing forth the fruits thereof.

37 And whoever challenges the faithful of this stone, will be broken, but upon whom ever it falls, it will grind them to powder."   (*Note* in Index)

38 When the chief priests, elders and Pharisees heard his parables, they perceived that he was talking about them.

39 But when they thought about laying their hands on him, they feared the multitude of disciples that believed in him as a prophet.

Note Verse 12

The attitude given Jesus with a fig tree is inappropriate in this verse. Fruit trees are "known" to go barren, thus ending their cycle of being any good at bearing fruit again. The improper attitude given here, is that because Jesus was hungry and it bore no fruit, he took out his frustration on the fig tree, which is NOT what "happened." He "saw" the tree and what condition it was in and that it was not good for what it was made.

Note Verses 37 to 39

The "STONE" Jesus SPEAKS "of" was discovered in 1799. The ROSETTA STONE. THAT which REVEALS the Kingdom of AMEN, his "FATHER." Known at the time of Jesus, and known to the disciples of Theban faith, this "stone" is the KEY to the "sacred" language of hieroglyphics. Since it is rejected by the Jewish peoples, Jesus is saying that Kingdom of Amen (Lord) will be taken from them and given to a nation which bears fruit unto the kingdom and those who go "against" those of the stone, will suffer the consequences for it. A prophesy made by Yeshua (Jesus) which "happened" and that "nation" was AMERICA. "Happened" as many of the "forefathers" of this country in it's beginnings were "Thebans. "That which is said to have been the SECRET SOCIETY. No secret that Roman Catholic Church leadership has this delusional idea that over the last two thousand years "they" are the chosen "nation/church" of most holy one and is why we hear their opinions on everything whether we are catholic or not and why many in their leadership have been "murderers." Bad leaders and clergy exemplify what Jesus said of the "blind."

Matt 15:14 ;

Let them alone: they be blind leaders of the blind. And if the blind lead the blind: both shall fall into the ditch. (KJV)

111

CHAPTER 23

1 Again, Jesus spoke to them in parables, saying,

2 "The kingdom of heaven is like a certain king, who made a marriage for his son,

3 He sent forth his servants to call on those who were invited to the wedding but they would not attend,

4 Later, he sent servants out for the second time, but told them, 'Tell those who have been invited that I have prepared a big dinner, having slaughtered oxen and fatlings for it and that everything is ready for them when they get here for the wedding ceremony.'

5 But it didn't matter to the persons who were invited and went about their business going their separate ways, one to his farm, another to his store,

6 And the rest of them took his servants, treating them spitefully, and killed them.

7 When the king heard what happened to his servants, he was very angry, and sent out his armies, destroyed those murderers and burned down their city.

8 Then he said to the rest of his servants, 'the wedding ceremony and feast is ready, but those who were invited aren't worthy to attend.'

9 Go instead upon the highways and invite as many as you can find to come to the wedding.'

10 So those servants went out into the highways, gathering together as many as could find, good and bad, and the wedding was furnished with those guests.

11 When the king came in to those invited amongst guests, he saw a man there who wasn't wearing wedding attire,

12 And he said to the man, 'Friend, how come you didn't dress up properly for the wedding occasion?' The man just stood there, speechless.

13 Then the king said to the servants, 'Bind him hand and foot and take him away and cast him into darkness to suffer the consequences of his decisions.

14 For many are called, but few are chosen.'"

15 Then the Pharisees went out to counsel amongst themselves to come up with a way to trap him with his own words.

16 After discussing the matter, the Pharisees sent some of their disciples along with Herodians to confront Jesus. Then they asked, "Master, we know that you are honest and teach the ways of the Lord in truth, nor do you care about the desires of man, for you don't follow after the ways of men.

17 Tell us then, what your opinion of what we ask? Is it lawful to give tribute to Caesar, or is it unlawful?"

18 But Jesus perceived their wickedness and said, "Why do you tempt me, with this question, you hypocrites.

19 Show me your tribute money." And they brought him a penny.

20 Jesus looked at the coin and said, "Whose is this image and inscription upon the coin?"

21 They answered, "Caesar's." Then Jesus took the coin and handed it back to them and said, "Then render unto Caesar the things which are Caesar's, and unto the Lord in heaven, the things that are his."

22 When they heard these words, they marveled at his wisdom, disappointingly left, and returned to those who sent them.

23 That same day came the Sadducees up to Jesus, a sect who say they don't believe in the resurrection and asked him,

24 "Master. Moses said, If a man dies never having wrought children into the world with his wife, his brother should marry his wife, and raise up seed unto his brother.

25 Now amongst us, were seven brothers, the first was married to a woman who didn't have children, so he left his wife to another brother,

26 Likewise the second died too, not having had children by this woman, who also left his wife to the third brother, and so on, until all seven brothers had been a husband to this woman who never bore any of them children.

27 After the seventh brother died, this woman later died, too.

28 Therefore if there is a resurrection, whose wife will she be in the afterlife, of the seven brothers, seeing all seven were married to her?

29 Jesus answered them and said, "You make a mistake by not knowing the scrip-

113

tures, nor the powers of Amen.

30 For in the resurrection no one is married, nor is anyone given into marriage, but are spirit and as the angels of Amen in heaven.

31 But on the subject of the resurrection of the dead, haven't you read that which was written within your own doctrines of Yahveh, stating,

32 'I am the Lord of Abraham, the Lord of Isaac, and the Lord of Jacob?' The Father in heaven is not the the Lord of the dead, but of the living."

33 When the Sadducees heard this, they were astonished of his doctrines.

34 But when the Pharisees heard that he had put the Sadducees to silence, they gathered together to discuss the matter.

35 Then one of them who was a lawyer, went up to Jesus and asked him a question, hoping to tempt him, and said,

36 "Master, which one is the great commandment in the our laws?"

37 Jesus replied, "'You should love the Lord in heaven with all your heart, soul and mind.'

38 This is the first and great commandment.

39 The second is like it, 'You should love your neighbor as you love yourself.'

40 Your law and prophets worthiness to heaven, depend on these two commandments."

41 While the Pharisees were still gathered together, Jesus asked them,
(*Note* in Index)

42 "What do you think of me? Whose son am I?" They replied, "The Son of David."

43 Then Jesus told them, "How then is it that David in spirit calls him Lord, saying,

44 The LORD said to my Lord, 'You sit down at my right hand, until I make your enemies your footstool?'

45 If your ancestor King David calls him Lord, which happens to be me, how can I be his son?"

46 Nobody was able to answer his analogy of himself to them, nor did they dare ask him any more questions after this day.

Note verses 41 - 46

The "biggest" misperceived TRUTH Jesus taught, and not understood within Judeo-Christianity, nor "accepted." Jewish descendants accept that Jesus was not their "messiah" nor was he a "descendant" of their cherished Judean King, David. Jesus or "Yeshua" WAS the "God" they believe to be Jehovah or "YAHVEH," come to them in the FLESH. He who was THOTH to the ancient Egyptians. The point of arbitration many Judeo-Christians have in Jesus being the Son of David is that all mankind descended from "Adam and Eve" in their beliefs, not SUBSTANTIATED by EVIDENCE or HISTORY. The one history record that pre-dates Judaism of creation is written "similar" to the Adam and Eve story, but does not degrade the role of women, as the "blame" for mankind's fall from Amen's GRACE. The Egyptian depiction of creation tells of Keb, much like Adam, was created from the earth. Nut, or the "Eve" of the story, was a "Goddess." The lines of CREATION to Egyptians follows BOTH the evolutionary lines of creation AND a SPIRITUAL "part" given by the Lord in heaven. Keb of earth, Nut from heaven. BODY and SOUL. In the Jewish depiction of creation, mankind is of the EARTH with NO spiritual connection to Amen in heaven. Adam of the dust of the ground, Eve created from his "rib." GENETICALLY, "wrong" as Adam and Eve would be brother and sister, and mankind as such created out of the act of INCEST. Though the children of the Goddess Nut and man of earth Keb, which are five of them, do MARRY each other except for Horus, mankind is created of the "flesh" and "spirit" NOT just the " FLESH. " Jesus never accepted being called SON OF DAVID, and he made it CLEAR " why. " King David was NOT "obedient" to Yahveh, nor was he a good example to his peoples. He was behaviorally inadequate to his faith and Jesus did not like being connected to him. King David before he died was silenced by his God in heaven for his disobedience and replaced by Solomon as King. In these verses Jesus makes it clear that "David" serves a " different " LORD, and that Lord is "subordinate," and makes it "clear" he IS, for David did not serve any God but HIMSELF. To clarify what is written on line four of this paragraph about Jesus being "Yahweh/Yahveh," he makes this "clear" that he IS the God the Jewish people worship as their "God" but only in NAME, for their PRACTICES are not up to the standards of HEAVEN. It is the one reason Jesus made reference to the fact "it was not so in the BEGINNING." The Hebrew peoples (Jewish), whether they like it or not were the PEOPLES, in ancient times who WERE chosen by Amen in heaven to continue in the faith he gave in the beginning for a Pharaoh abolished it within Egypt during his reign. (Akhenaton) Problem IS, that soon AFTER the faithful of Amen amongst the Hebrews AGAIN fell from his grace by CHANGING many of his "truths" with vain pursuits. "LORD'S" are they who are AS the creator in heaven, and as such is JESUS. The "Lord" of EARTH or "MEDIATOR" of the peoples of THIS planet and species.

Note

Before I go into Chapter 24, one of the things that should be noted within all that was ever written about Jesus, much of his "personal" life is left out. From one chapter to the next, he is "speaking" or "healing" and very little is ever said about everyday living. If any of us lived the kind of life depicted by the books written about Jesus we would be "bored." No humor, and everything written in a serious tone. Jesus was a very "open" person, and from all that is written of a NATURE which no religion has perceived in proper form because of the "God" he is said to represent. PERCEIVED, because the nature of Jesus was not of THIS world, "thus" not put in proper perspective. Not even the Apostles Jesus chose on earth, perceived his nature and how that is evident is by the examples that are written of various incidents involving some of the Apostles. Of those written involved brothers James and John, Peter, Phillip, and Thomas. Though these five required "proof" Jesus was the Lord at one time or another or denied him at one time or another, the only apostle who was not put to death out of all the apostles was, John, but he lived a long and hard life, and much of that was to learn humility, of which he never learned. Many Judeo-Christians cherish the works of the Apostle John and in every New Testament are "5" of his books. "Simon Peter" though, "was" much "closer" to Jesus and curiously one of his major books is left out of present day bibles, not accepted, or "canonized." Peter was, as any scholar can verify, a close "student" to Jesus and was chastised and taught personally by Jesus, though he later is devoutly "Jewish," in his beliefs that Gentiles were not "worthy" to receive the teachings of Christ. Though it is said that it is the reason Jesus chose Saul (the Apostle Paul), to the "astute" scholar reading all Jesus taught, he DID say that he particularly came unto the Jews, which Peter adhered to until Paul told him "his" purpose, and the will of Christ.

ACTS 13:45 – 46

But when the Jews saw the multitudes, they were filled with envy, and spake against those things which were spoken by Paul, contradicting and blaspheming. Then Paul and Barnabas waxed bold, and said, "It was necessary that the word of

117

the Lord should first have been spoken to you but seeing ye put it from you, and judge yourselves unworthy of everlasting life, lo, we turn to the Gentiles." (KJV)

"Originally" Jesus came "specifically" unto the Jewish peoples. Several of the most important FACTS escapes Judeo-Christianity in their faith in Jesus. As I already stated, one of them is his NATURE. PASSIVE. Assertive, critical, judgmental, and truthful, but yet "passive" is what lead to his dilemma where he was eventually crucified, but the most important behavioral aspect missed out of everything taught by Judeo-Christianity is what was done to Sodom and Gommorrah within Jewish faith, not to mention countless other incidents within Jewish beliefs that lead to their beliefs in a God of Wrath. Jesus could have done the same, and destroyed Jerusalem. Did he? Why?, it was within his powers. The neglect to examine many attributes of the nature and character of Jesus, including his "faith," is what has lead to the confusion of modern Christianity and why it remains a TWO-FOLD indoctrinated mire of blasphemies made up by men who vainly killed off all those of truth within the first 100 years and continued to go after every sect that did not agree with the church brought about by the Roman Empire. Of course, I have gotten in many debates with other scholars because Emperor Constantine and his mother "proclaimed" to be "Christians" but as Jesus said,

"Wherefore by their fruits ye shall know them." (KJV)

It was the "Romans" who went after disciples of Jesus throughout their Empire, and "beyond." When it's empire fell in the 6th century, the slaughters did not stop with these emperors, it became the endeavor of the church it helped create for the next "13" centuries. The "FRUITS," are "obvious," as are the "fruits" of the Jewish religion and it's leaders Jesus chastised many times over their behaviors. KILLING, in any way, shape or form for whatever REASON, is NOT of the Kingdom of heaven, for it is not of it's NATURE or the nature of the HOLY. Another FACT Judeo-Christians miss about who will be WORTHY, is what Jesus SAID about, BLASPHEMY.

118

Matthew 12:31

"Wherefore I say unto you, All manner of sin and blasphemy shall be forgiven unto men, but the blasphemy against the Holy Ghost shall not be forgiven unto men."

(KJV)

The "obvious" factor which is not examined within all of earth's present religions, which "WAS," in ancient Theban faith, was RESPECT, for all living creatures, including our own. Whether Jesus is one thing or another in Christianity to achieve "holiness," whether Mohammad is one thing or another within Islam to achieve "holiness," whether Jehovah is one thing or another to Jews to achieve "holiness," means NOTHING when people of ANY religion EXECUTE, KILL, PERSECUTE and "adhere" to principles that ANIMALS live by, living in FEAR and THOUGHT of selfish desires meant to please one's self at the cost of the lives of other living creatures. It is THIS "respect," for life that eventually lead to the fall of the "native" Egyptian Pharaohs, and I am NOT including all the "invaders" and "conquerors" written about by the ancient Hebrews who did NOT go into detail when it came to their hatred of Egypt's rulers, except in all that was written around the Babylonian captivity. Egypt had NO "native" Pharaohs after 1080 b.c., except for one in the 4th century b.c. All the rest had been FOREIGNER rulers who also called themselves PHAROAHS, "unworthy" of the "title."

Another FACT any person should remember is, that whatever has been ANY act of violence or murderers upon the innocent ARE of the "past" and the GUILTY for those acts are NOT the descendants of any culture, religion or person(s). The only "way" that peace can ever be achieved in the world, is to let "ignorance" itself be part of the past. The most important part of "wisdom" is to gain an intellect that surpasses emotion which "practices" what Jesus taught. Love for enemies, which goes not just into the "present," but the past as well. Whatever peoples of religions, cultures, etc., have done in the past is NOT the responsibility of the "descendants" to pay a price for. The one ludicrous act I have encountered is the one of prejudice of a peoples or religion for the behaviors of the past. Nothing "present" in the world is

119

"guilty" for anything of the past and it is not up to "us" to judge anyone. That "judgment" is the Lord in heaven's job, and his "alone......."

CHAPTER 24

1 Jesus then turned to the multitude of peoples there and his disciples,

2 And said, "The scribes and the Pharisees sit in Moses' seat,

3 Therefore, everything they tell you to observe, do, but don't do the follow after their ways because they tell you what should be done but don't do it themselves,

4 They tell people they must do hard work for them and assign it to them but they themselves won't lift a finger to help,

5 They like to do things for others with what they get from you for free so as to be seen by those around them, then pray out in the open with their broad phylacteries around their foreheads even going as far as enlarging the borders of their garments,

6 They love to demand the uppermost rooms at feasts, and the chief seats in the synagogues,

7 And act important in the markets enjoying the attention they get from everyone who calls them, Rabbi, Rabbi,

8 But don't allow yourselves to be called Rabbi, for there is but one Rabbi, the Lord in heaven,

9 Don't let any person call you Father upon the earth, for there is but one Father in heaven and all of you are his family,

10 Neither, let any person call you master, for there also, is only one, and he is the Master of all things on earth and in heaven,

11 The greatest amongst you, should serve the rest of you,

12 And who ever is full of pride in themselves, should be abased, and the persons who live in humility and are humble, should be exalted,

13 But woe unto you, scribes and Pharisees, you hypocrites!, for you will be shut out of the kingdom of heaven, for you don't bother to do the things that will make you worthy of it and restrain your followers from entering also,

14 Woe unto you, scribes and Pharisees, you hypocrites!, for you swallow up the possessions of widows' and pray long prayer pretending it's for them and for what

you steal from the less fortunate, you will pay the price, receiving a greater damnation,

15 Woe unto you, scribes and Pharisees, you hypocrites! for you will cross land and sea to bring one convert into your fold, and when you have accomplished converting that person over to your religion you make that person, twice as bad a child of hell than you are,

16 Woe unto you, you blind guides, who say, 'Who ever will swear by the temple, it is nothing, but whoever swears by the gold of the temple, owes the temple a debt!,'

17 You fools and blind hypocrites, for which is greater, the gold, or the temple that sanctifies the gold?,

18 You say, 'Who ever shall swear by the altar, it is nothing, but whoever swears by the gift that is upon it, he is guilty,'

19 You fools and blind hypocrites, for which is greater, the gift, or the altar that sanctifies the gift?,

20 Who ever then swears by the altar, swears by it and all things upon it,

21 Who ever swears by the temple, swears by it and by those who dwell inside,

22 And the person who swears by heaven, swears by the throne of Amen and by him that sits upon that throne,

23 Woe unto you, scribes and Pharisees, you hypocrites!, for you pay tithe of mint, anise and cumin, omitting the guilt of the heavier matters of the law, judgment, mercy, and faith. You should have done these things 'first,' before leaving them undone thinking your tithe will make up for your neglect,

24 You blind guides, who criticize small things but don't look at the big errors of your ways,

25 Woe unto you, scribes and Pharisees, you hypocrites!, for you clean and groom yourselves like you clean the outside of a cup and platter, but within you, you are full of extortions and so many wrongful behaviors to mention,

26 You blind Pharisees, first clean your behaviors from the inside like you clean that cup and platter, that the outside of you may be clean also,

27 Woe unto you, scribes and Pharisees, you hypocrites!, for you like the white sepulchers, which indeed appear beautiful on the outside, but within are full of dead peoples bones and their uncleanness,

28 Even so are all of you, who outwardly appear righteous unto everyone but within you, all of you are full of hypocrisies and wickedness (iniquity),

29 Woe unto you, scribes and Pharisees, you hypocrites!, for you build the tombs of prophets, and garnish the sepulchers of the righteous,

30 And say, 'If we had lived in the days of our forefathers, we wouldn't have been taken part with those who killed the prophets,'

31 Wherefore you be your own witnesses, for you are the children of those people who killed the prophets,

32 And with the measure you have judged should have been paid by your forefathers , judge unto yourselves,

33 You serpents, you generation of vipers, how can you escape the damnations of hell?,

34 Wherefore, look for yourselves, I send unto you prophets, wise men, and scribes. Some of them you will kill and crucify, and some of them, you will scourge in your synagogues, persecuting them from city to city,   (*Note* in Index)

35 That upon you may come a curse of all the righteous blood shed upon the earth, from the blood of righteous Abel unto the blood of Zacharias, son of Barachias, whom you slew between the temple and the altar,

36 Amen-Ra says to tell you, All these things will come upon this generation,

37 Oh, Jerusalem, Jerusalem, your people who kills the prophets and stones thoses sent to you. How often would I have gathered your children together, even as a hen gathers her chicks under her wings, and you would not!,

38 Look for yourselves, your house is left desolate unto you,

39 For I say unto you, You will not see me again after this day until you shall say, 'Blessed is he that cometh in the name of the Lord.'"

Note Verses 34 - 39

Verifies what I wrote about Jesus, being Yahveh in the flesh and did not appreciate 2000 years ago being called the hebrew God. He "abolished" his position, with the ending statement in verse 39, "You will not see me again after this day until you shall say, 'Blessed is he that cometh in the name of the Lord.'" These verses explain "who" Jesus IS, but has been look over by the masses. In the ANCIENT FAITH given by Amen in heaven, the GENERAL terminology of the holy to live on earth in the "flesh" amongst this species has been to be called a Son of Amen or the Lord, of which Pharoahs called themselves. Jesus though was a PHYSICAL "creation" in the flesh of a SPIRIT (God) who had been "appointed" by the Lord of Creation in the BEGINNING, called "Yahweh," and over mankind's "existance" has been in the "flesh" amongst mankind more times than "one," but because mankind can not fully "comprehend" the holy in heaven, they can not comprehend spiritual IMMORTAL-ITY. In verse 37 he says, "How often would I have gathered your children together, even as a hen gathers her chicks under her wings, and you would not!," How "often" (more than one time), not "if" I would gather, but how "often" WOULD "I" have gathered. As SPIRIT, the man many knew as Yeshua in Israel, now called Jesus, has not only come amongst mankind 2000 years, but many times to various "cultures" in the FLESH, and not just in the "male" form, but "female" as well. SEX nor GENDER is PART of HEAVEN, "even" when the spirits come in fleshly form, for they are not HINDERED by "ignorance" OR "emotions" as the homo-sapien species IS. It is what distinguishes the INTELLIGENT from the IGNORANT. Holy books of every religion but ONE, DENY the INTELLIGENCE of the holy in heaven and how they do this, is by CATAGORIZING "the Lord in heaven" as being weak in character and behaviors as mankind on this planet. Hebrews did this repeatedly, beginning with their depiction of creation of man and woman in Bereshis. (Genesis) Woman created out of the rib of Man. Here is a "story" of the Almighty Lord in heaven who supposed-ly has the power to create all things living from scratch, yet resorts to creating a woman from "spare parts." The rib of Adam. It will anger the Jews of modern day, but it SHOULD anger them ENOUGH to look at all the ignorance of their forefathers which has INSULTED the holy in heaven, for it is BLASPHEMY to attach such inferior behaviors upon his holiness in heaven and TEACH that this is the ways he is, when he is NOT. Just as the Jews insulted and eventually KILLED Jesus in his day for wanting to CORRECT them, he is NOT the only one religions have done this to. Religions have done it to MILLIONS, and it is the "blasphemy" that has infected the doctrines given mankind of a kind, compassionate, loving, caring Lord in heaven.

CHAPTER 25

1 After he was done talking, Jesus went out and departed from the temple. As he was leaving the Apostles came up to him wanting him to view the buildings around the temple.

2 And Jesus said to them, "You see all these buildings?, Amen-Ra says to tell you, there won't be one stone left here upon another, for it will be torn down."

3 As they walked, they came to the Mount of Olives where Jesus sat down, where again, the Apostles came up to him, only this time in private, asking, "Tell us, when will the things that you are telling us come about?, and what will be the signs of the you returning to earth and the end of the world?"

4 Jesus answered them, "Watch out that nobody deceives you,

5 For many will come in my name, saying, 'I am Christ, messiah of the Jews, when you know I am the divine one, foretold in Egyptian sacred papyri, come for 'all' mankind, not just Jews. These other ones will deceive many by their doctrines.

6 You will hear of wars and rumors of wars, but see that you don't worry about it for all these things must come to pass but the end is not yet.

7 Nation shall rise against nation, and kingdom against kingdom, and there will be famines, pestilences, and earthquakes in divers places.

8 All these are the beginning of sorrows.

9 Then the unfaithful will deliver you up to be tortured, to kill you and you will be hated of all nations for my name's sake.

10 Many will be offended by these truths, betray one another, and will hate one another because of them.

11 Many false prophets will rise up and will deceive many.

12 And because of the iniquity of these deceivers of religions who use my name will be many, love of many will be non-existent.

13 But the person who endures in faith till they pass from this world, will be saved.

14 This gospel of the kingdom will be preached in all parts of the world for a witness to all nations, and then the end of the deceivers will come.

15 When you see the abomination of desolation, written in the book of the Hebrew prophet Daniel come about in Jerusalem, who ever reads this let them understand, (*Note* in Index)

16 Then let everyone in Israel flee into the mountains,

17 Those on the roofs jump off and leave forgetting their belongings in the house,

18 The one in the field, not return home to gather clothes,

19 And have pity for the women who are with child, and to them that are nursing a baby in those days!

20 Pray that your escape is not in the winter or on the sabbath day,

21 For there will be great hardships, the likes of which have never been felt by anyone since the beginning of the world unto this day, no, hardships that no one has felt before.

22 Unless your flesh dies soon after these days start, the rest will suffer in agony until they are destroyed, but for the faithful, they will leave this world first so none will suffer.

23 If anyone says to you,'Here is Jesus, or there he is, don't believe it.

24 Close to the end, there will rise false teachers, false prophets, showing all kinds of great signs and wonders, so much so, that if it possible, they will deceive those of you who know these truths.

25 Beware, for I have told you before.

26 Don't listen to their deceptions, so be alert, for they will try to convince you I am come in the desert, or in secret chambers, so beware of these deceivers and don't believe in their lies.

27 For as lightning comes without notice, so will it be when I return unto humanity.

28 For wherever death is, there you will find all the vultures gathered together.

29 Immediately after the hardships of these days, the sun be darkened, the moon will not shine, stars will shoot across the sky, and the planets in space will be shaken,

30 Then shall appear the sign of my return from heaven and then will all the unfaithful throughout the earth will mourn for they will see me coming upon the clouds of heaven with great power and glory.

31 Then will I send out my angels ahead of me in a great sound to gather my faithful from one end of space to the other.

32 Now learn a parable of the fig tree, When it's branch is yet tender and putting forth buds that grow into leaves, you know that summer is close,

33 So in comparison, when you see all these things happen, know that these things I have told you are about to happen, so close, they are at the door.

34 Amen-Ra says to tell you, This generation will not die until all these things come about.　　　　(*Note* in Index)

35 Heaven and earth will cease to exist, but my words will never die.

36 But of that day and hour when I am dead, risen, and return from heaven, nobody knows, not even the angels of heaven. Only my Father knows when that will happen.

37 But as in the days of the great flood came so unexpected, so will it be when I return from heaven.

38 For as in the great flood, everyone went about their business, eating, drinking, marrying, being given unto marriage, (*Note* in Index)

39 Because nobody knew that a flood was about to occur and killed them all, so suddenly will it be like this flood when I return.

40 Of two who are out in the field working, one will be taken who is faithful while the other one who is not, will be left behind.

41 Two women will be grinding at the mill, one who is faithful will be taken while the unfaithful one will be left behind.

42 Watch then once I am gone, for you won't know the day or hour when your Lord will return unto you.

43 But know this, that if the good man of the house had known in what watch the thief would come, he would have watched and would not have suffered his house to be destroyed and robbed.

44 Therefore stay alert once I am gone for in the time when you don't think I will return, I will come.

45 Who then will be a faithful and wise disciple, whom this lord has made ruler over

his doctrines, to teach them to those who yearn to learn them?

46 Blessed is the disciple who, when this lord returns, finds his faithful busy doing the things he asked.

47 Amen-Ra says to tell you, That I will make them rulers over all I have.

48 But if the evil disciple says in their heart, 'The Lord delays his coming,

49 So I don't have to do my part, goes into abusing people, behaving badly, and abusing drugs or drinking alcohol too much,

50 I will come in that day that disciple doesn't expect it, or an hour unknown to them,

51 And will get rid of them, giving them their portion of damnation they deserve along with the rest of the hypocrites, where the irrational belong.

INDEX*CHAPTER 25

***Note* Verses 15**

The Hebrew prophet Daniel "wept" over the vision he was given. Wept, because despite Judeo-Christian beliefs in the coming of a "New Jerusalem" in end times, all of what Jesus "said" has nothing to do with an "end of the world" scenario. The "abomination of desolation" he is referring to in this Chapter is, that GRACE, is no longer of a God for the Jews, for they have strayed far from the truth and will from his day forward be left to their "hypocrisies." Left to the will of the devil. It is what Daniel "saw" and why he wept.

***Note* Verses 34**

In Judeo-Christianity, many of them are "still" looking for the day Jesus "returns." He "already" HAS. THREE DAYS AFTER HE WAS CRUCIFIED. He said in this verse, "THIS GENERATION WILL NOT 'DIE' (pass away) until these things come about.," NOT "these things will happen AGAIN after my ascension."
Everything in this CHAPTER has already taken place, after Jesus was crucified. The sun darked, moon didn't shine etc. Read Matthew 27:45 - 28:10.

***Note* Verses 38**

The story of Noah in present times is "known" to have been from the Epic of Gilgamesh. Of Mesopotamian origin and not "Jewish." There was a Great Flood at one time in the region, but NOT a "world" incident. The "Noah" story is "literature" ADDED to an event that took place but on a local level, MATHEMATICALLY improbable, and ILLOGICAL for any man to achieve such a feat as to collect two of every species on earth and on top of that, to BUILD a vessel large enough to house or "feed" them for the length of time told in this story. I raise "dogs" and each and everyday use 12 pounds of food just for them. Imagine feeding "thousands" of creatures and then the "excrement" from them for 204 days or 6 months 24 days approximately, as told in the story. The whole story is so RIDICULOUS I am surprised anyone BELIEVES IT, but yet many do, so much so, as to spend millions on expeditions to FIND the ARK. Wonder how many children all this wasted money might have fed were it used on the REALITIES, and not on proving what simple math equates, and simple behavioral evaluation of the Lord's nature would tell any intelligent reader it is "fiction."

CHAPTER 26

1 I compare the kingdom of heaven to ten virgins who took ten lamps to have with them when they met the bridegroom.

2 Five of them were wise, and five were foolish.

3 The ones who were foolish, took their lamps but forgot to take oil with them,

4 The wise ones, though, took oil in their vessels for their lamps.

5 While they waited for the bridegroom to show up, all of them got tired of waiting and went to sleep,

6 At midnight someone cried out to the virgins, Behold, the bridegroom is coming, go out to meet him.

7 Then the wise virgins got up, and took their lamps, which were still lit.

8 But the foolish ones said unto the wise ones, 'Give us some of your oil, as our lamps have gone out.'

9 But the wise virgins said, 'We can't, since there isn't enough for the five of us and you too, but go out to those who sell oil and buy some for yourselves.'

10 The foolish virgins went out to buy oil for their lamps, but while they were out the bridegroom came, and the five wise virgins went with him to the wedding and locked the door behind them.

11 When the foolish virgins found out the bridegroom showed up while they were gone, they went to the place where the wedding was to take place and said, 'Lord, Lord, open the door to us.'

12 But he answered and said, 'Amen-Ra says, I don't know who you are.'

13 Watch therefore, for you won't know the day nor the hour I return unto you.'

14 I also compare the kingdom of heaven to a man who was traveling to a far off country so he called to three of his servants to bring him the things he was taking with him.

15 When they finished bringing him his goods, he gave one of the servants five talents, another two talents and the last one, one talent, entrusting the money to them to hold for him, then left on his journey.

16 The servant to whom was given five talents, went out and used his money to trade with and earned an additional five talents.

17 Like that servant, the one who was given two talents went out and also gained an additional two talents.

18 But the servant who was paid one talent, went out and buried it, hiding the money he was paid.

19 After a long time, the lord of those servants returned home and called in these three servants.

20 The servant he had given five talents came and showed him that he made an additional five talents saying, 'Lord, you gave me five talents and look, I went out and earned an additional five talents with it.'

21 His lord said to him, 'Well done, my good and faithful servant, you have done good with what little I entrusted unto you, enter into the joys of your lord for I will make you ruler over many things.

22 The second servant whom he had given two talents, also came up to him and said, "Lord, you gave me two talents and look, I have gained an additional two talents besides the ones you gave me.'

23 His lord said to him, 'Well done, my good and faithful servant, you have done good with what little I entrusted unto you, enter into the joys of your lord for I will make you ruler over many things.

24 Then the third servant who received only one talent came up to him and said, 'Lord, I know you are a hard man, reaping where you have not sown, and gathering where you have not worked,

25 And was afraid to anger you so I went out and hid the talent you gave me in the earth so I could return it to you when you returned.

26 His lord replied, 'You wicked and lazy servant, you knew that I reap where I don't sow, and gather where I have haven't worked,

27 But you should have used the money I gave you to put to the exchangers, and then when I returned I should have received my money with interest.

28 Take the talent from this servant and give it to the one who has ten.

29 For everyone that has faith, will receive even more, and will always have confidence, but for the one who does nothing with the faith I give unto them to add unto the kingdom, that faith which they do nothing with will be taken away from them.

30 And will be considered worthless, unto the kingdom of heaven.

31 When I return in all my glory, and all the holy angels with me, then will they who profit the kingdom sit along side me on their thrones in glory,

32 Before me will be gathered all persons from every nation, and I will separate them one from another, as a shepherd divides his sheep from the goats,

33 And I will set the sheep who are the righteous on my right hand, while I set the goats, who are the unrighteous to the left.

34 Then will I say to those at my right hand, Come, for you are the blessed of my Father in heaven, you inherit the kingdom prepared for you from the beginning,

35 For I was hungry, and you fed me, I was thirsty, and you gave me something to drink, I was a stranger, and you took me in,

36 Naked, and you clothed me, I was sick, and you visited me, I was in prison, and you came to see me.

Note Verses 14 - 30

Parable of the Lord and three servants written in "proper" perspective as the translation left the "original" story punishing the servant entrusted with one talent, and the parable as though Jesus took sides with the issue of "money." Money was not the reason for the parable, of which I have seen many Judeo-Christians think the parable is about. The parable was meant to fortify "testimony" amongst the disciples, or THEY who are entrusted with wisdom, should use it to teach with to get others to also be wise in faith. I have seen many churches take this parable to mean when tithes are given, they should use it to "multiply" the proceeds into "more" money for the church. Totally FALSE.

CHAPTER 27

1 Then the righteous asked him, "Lord, when did we see you hungry, and feed you, thirsty, and gave you something to drink?"

2 When did we see you as a stranger, and took you in, naked, and clothed you?

3 Or when did we see you sick, in prison, and came to help you?"

4 And Jesus answered, "Amen-Ra says to tell you, In as much as you have done it unto the least of one amongst you, you have done it unto me."

5 Then Jesus will say unto these, come unto me on my right hand and unto those who are selfish, "Depart from me, you who live by the ways of your father for you are cursed in everlasting damnation, prepare for the devil and his angels,

6 For when I was hungry, you did not feed me, when I was thirsty, you gave me nothing to drink,

7 I was a stranger, and you turned me away, I was naked, and you wouldn't give me a stitch of clothing to cover myself, in prison, and you didn't even visit me.

8 Then they will ask, "Lord, when did we see you hungry, thirsty, a stranger, naked, sick, or in prison, and did not attend to your needs?"

9 Then I will answer them, "Amen-Ra says to tell you, In as much as you do not do these simple things amongst each other even amongst the least of you, you do it, as though you have done it unto me.

10 These kind of persons are as their father, who take but will not give, and if they will not give even of the simplest of things, how can they expect the Father in heaven to give them life eternal where the righteous all help each other in unity?" (*Note* in Index)

11 When Jesus finished his teachings, he said to his apostles and disciples,

12 "You know that in two days after the feast of the passover, I will be betrayed and turned over to be crucified."

13 On one of the days of the passover, the chief priests, scribes and elders of the peoples assembled together at the palace of the high priest, who was called Caiaphas,

14 Together they discussed how they might apprehend Jesus without detection to kill him.

15 But concluded that they should not do it on the feast day, fearing it might create a riot amongst his disciples,

16 Jesus went unto Bethany to the house of Simon the leper,

17 While there, a woman came unto him with an alabaster box, filled with very precious ointment and poured it on his head as he sat down to eat,

18 When the apostles saw her doing this, they got angry and said, "To what purpose is this waste?

19 This ointment is very expensive and could have been sold and the money given to the poor."

20 When Jesus heard them, he said, "Why are you bothering this woman, don't you see is doing something good for me?

21 You will always have poor people amongst you, but I won't be around with you too much longer.

22 For in pouring this ointment on my body, she has done it to prepare me for my burial.

23 Amen-Ra says to tell you, Wherever this gospel is preached in world, there will also be this event told of what this woman has done this day to remember her by as a memorial.

24 At about the same time Judas Iscariot, who was one of the twelve apostles, went to see the chief Jewish priests,

25 While there he asked them, "What will you give me if I deliver Jesus into your hands?" They finally agreed upon thirty pieces of silver.

26 After this day, Judas sought an opportunity to betray him and turn him over to the authorities who paid him for it.

27 On the first day of the feast of unleavened bread, the apostles came up to Jesus and asked, "Where are we going to prepare for you the passover meal?"

28 Jesus replied, "Go into the city to this one disciple and tell him that I say my time is at hand and I will keep the passover at eat at his house with you, my

apostles."

29 And the apostles did as Jesus asked them to and later went to the man's house to prepare the passover meal.

30 That evening, Jesus sat down with the twelve apostles at the table.

31 And as they ate, Jesus said, "Amen-Ra says to tell you, one of you has already betrayed me."

32 Looking at each other, the apostles exceeding sorrowful, began one by one to ask, "Lord, is it me?"

33 Then Jesus answered and said, "The one who just dipped his hand in the dish with mine, is the one who has betrayed me,

34 And I have done as written of me, by the prophets of Hebrews and prophets of Egyptians, but not even the Son of Amen is important enough that he too is not betrayed by one of his closest."

35 Then Judas, who betrayed him said, "Master, is it me?" And Jesus said, "So you just said." Judas, got up and left.

36 As they continued eating Jesus took the bread, blessed it and broke it into portions for all of them, giving each apostle there a piece and said, "Take and eat this bread for it represents my body."   (*Note* in Index)

37 Then he took the vessel of wine and filled each of their cups, gave thanks and said, "Drink all of it,

38 For this represents my blood which will be spilled by men, and as Osiris refused life in the flesh after his murder, but rather to offer life eternal in the spirit to others, so do I, as many Pharaohs before me to offer it unto you.

39 I say unto you, I will not drink of the fruit of the vine from this day forward until that day when I will drink it new with you in my Father's kingdom.

40 When they were done with the meal, they sang a hymn and then went out into the Mount of Olives.

Note Verse 10

The Judeo-Christian translations always follow after the "persecuting" Jesus ideology, of which is the FALSE representation of how Jesus WAS. The disobedient don't NEED a Lord or even "mediator" to punish them as their own ignorance and behaviors give them a life of constant ups and downs they have to deal with. Amen in heaven contrary to religions and their "assumptions" of his nature, doesn't need to instill fear in the people of punishment or "hell" who will not follow his wisdom. The one FACT of TRUTH "is," that Jesus, just like Amen in heaven, warns people of what will happen if certain things are not done to assure spiritual peace. In the books of the Apostles written by Judeo-Christianity it is the one thing that makes it obvious much of their works were rewritten or written with the "God of Wrath" ideology which is FALSE.

Note Verses 36 - 39

Called the "LAST SUPPER." The reason so many of Jewish and Judeo-Christian religion can not DISCERN who Jesus WAS, is that few are EDUCATED in anything BUT their own doctrines. For 184 years, Egypt's doctrines of faith in their own religion have been out there for anyone to read. Amongst it's articles of faith, is the rite of Osiris. Where a GOD ON EARTH LAYS DOWN THEIR LIVES FOR THE SALVATION OF OTHERS FROM THE "DEVIL" TO GAIN THEM ETERNAL LIFE IN HEAVEN. Ritual performed since approximately 3400 b.c . - The King (God on Earth) who chose to lay down their lives for the peoples would take a piece of bread as a representation of their "body" and the people would eat, and to represent the blood shed for them, a cup of wine was the chosen drink. Then the King was "sacrificed" or "killed." This rite originated from the belief passed down that Seth (the serpent ; devil) killed his brother Osiris, who had been chosen by Amen to be the King on earth, but Seth was so jealous he MURDERED his brother and took his throne. Isis, wife of Osiris looked for the "pieces" of Osiris, as the devil or Seth had butchered him and sent parts to various places. (Reason band-ages used to wrap mummies) Once Isis found all the pieces of Osiris' body, she RESURRECTED him, only to find out that Osiris did not want to exist in the flesh, but in the spirit world or HEAVEN. So as to combat Seth in his evil ways, Osiris told Isis he would GUARD the afterlife from those of evil and to those found worthy he would be a "mediator" between Amen in heaven and savior to give them eternal life. Jesus was a "scholar" of man's and Amen's wisdom, and as in the faith of Egypt, 12 Apostles are as the "12" God's of the council in heaven, where there too, is taught that "one" of them was a "devil." Sound FAMILAR?

CHAPTER 28

1 Then Jesus said to his apostles, "All of you will feel insecure after this night, for in one of your books of Samuel it is written, 'And I will come upon him while he is weary and weak handed, and will make him afraid, and all the people that are with him shall flee, and I will smite the king only.   (*Note* in Index)

2 After I am risen again, I will go before you in Galilee.   (*Note* in Index)

3 Peter spoke up and said, "Though everyone will feel insecure and fearful of being persecuted like you will be, I won't be."

4 But Jesus said to Peter, "Amen-Ra says to tell you, that on this night before the rooster crows in the dawn, you will deny me three times.

5 But don't let your heart be troubled, for you believe in Amen and also believe in me."

6 Then Peter said unto Jesus, "Even though they put me to death with you, I won't deny you nor will any of the other apostles.

7 Jesus said, "In my Father's house are many mansions, if it were not so, I would have told you. I go to prepare a place for you." (The one KEY Jesus left his disciples as to WHO HE WAS and of what FAITH.   (*Note* in Index)

8 And if I go and prepare a place for you, I will come again, and receive you unto myself, that where I am, there ye may be also.

9 And where I go, you know, and the way, you also know."

10 Thomas asked him, "Lord, we don't know where you are going, so how can we know the way?"

11 Jesus answered him and said, "I am the way, the truth, and the life. No one comes unto the Father, except through me.

12 If you have known me, you have also known my Father, and from this day foreward, you know him and have seen him (in the flesh)."

13 Philip then asked him, "Lord, show us the Father that will be sufficient enough to convince us."

14 Jesus looked at Phillip and said, "Have I been with you so long that you have

not known who I am? Everyone who has seen me in the flesh, has also seen the Father in heaven, so how can you say, 'Show us the Father?'"

15 Don't you believe that I am in the Father, and the Father is in me? Everything I have taught you, came not out of me but the Father who dwells within me, for in spirit we are one."

16 Believe me when I say that I am in the Father, and the Father is in me, or if you have a hard time believing that, look at all the miracles and works done that only the Lord in heaven is capable of.

17 Amen-Ra says to tell you, verily that the person who believes on me for the works and miracles I have done, will do 'greater' works and miracles than these because I soon leave to be with my Father.

18 Whatsoever you ask in my name, that, will I do, that the Father may be glorified in the Son.

19 If you have need of anything, ask in my name and I will do it.

20 If you love me, keep the commandments I have taught you.

21 And I will pray the Father, and he will give you another Comforter, only a Holy Spirit unto each one of you that he may abide with you forever,

22 A Spirit of truth, whom the unfaithful of the world cannot receive, because they can not see them, nor do they know this gift unto the faithful, but you know the holy spirit, for it dwells with you, and will be in you.

23 I will not leave you without comfort when they subject my flesh to be put to death, for I will return unto you.

24 Yet in a little while, the world will see me no more, but you will see me, because I will live, just as you will live too.

25 On that day, you will know that I am in the Father, you in me, and I in you.

26 The person who has my commandments, and keeps them, is one who loves me, and the person that loves me, will be loved of my Father, just as I will love them and manifest myself to them."

27 Judas, not Judas Iscariot but a disciple, asked, "Lord, how is it that you will manifest yourself unto us, and not unto the unfaithful of the world?"

28 Jesus answered and said unto him, "If a person loves me, they will keep my teachings, and my Father will also love that person, for we will come to that person and always dwell in them through the holy spirit.

29 The person who does not love me, does not adhere to my teachings for they do not believe that the words I teach come from the Father who sent me.

30 These things, are things I have told you while yet present amongst you.

31 But the Comforter, which is the Holy Spirit, whom the Father will send unto you in my name, will teach you of all things and bring all these things I have taught you to refresh your memories of them so you don't forget.

32 Peace I leave with you, for the peace I have given you, is not as the world gives it, but as dwells in heaven, so don't let your hearts be troubled, nor allow yourselves to be afraid.

33 You have heard me say to you, I go away and come again unto you. If you love me, you should rejoice because I am going unto the Father in heaven who sent me , and my Father is greater than I am.

34 Now I have told you all these things before they happen so that when they do happen you will believe.

35 From here on, I will get the opportunity to talk to you much for the prince of this world is coming, who is the devil and has nothing in me.

36 For these things I do that the world may know that I love the Father, and as the Father gave me commandment, even so do I. Arise, lets leave this place, and take a walk.

Note Verse 1

Rewritten by Amen John I into proper recall within the Jewish scriptures.

Note Verse 2

"Unusual" Jesus tells the Apostles after he is crucified he will come unto them in "Galilee" and not Jerusalem, but part of the ministry of Jesus was not to "convince" the Gentiles of who he was, it was the hypocritical Jews that needed "proof." Three days later that proof was his resurrection.

Note Verse 7

Clearly shows that Jesus was teaching the "Egyptian" and not Jewish faith and "knew" the writings of the Book of the Dead.

In the Papyri of Nebseni, priest of Egypt is written this holy Sacrament ;
16:8 And there, in the heavenly MANSIONS of heaven which my divine father Amen has established, let my hands lay hold upon the wheat and the barley, which shall be given unto me therein in abundant measure, and may the SON of my own body make ready for me my food therein.

CHAPTER 29

1 As they walked, Jesus said to his apostles, "I am the true vine, and my Father is the caretaker,

2 Every branch in me that bears no fruit, he cuts and takes away. Every branch that bears fruit, he prunes that it may bring forth more fruit.

3 Now you are clean through the word which I have taught to you.

4 Abide in me, and I will abide in you. As the branch cannot bear fruit of itself unless it is attached to the vine, you can not bring others to the kingdom of heaven unless you abide in me.

5 I am the vine, you are the branches. The one that abides in me, while I abide in them that same person will bring forth much fruit for without me you can do nothing.

6 If a person does not abide in me, that person becomes like a barren branch which dries up, gathered up as useless and cast into the fire and burned.

7 If you abide in me, and my teachings abide in you, you will be able to ask what you will, and it shall be done unto you.

8 Herein is my Father glorified by you bringing many others into the family of the Lord in heaven, bearing much fruit unto him, as my apostles and disciples.

9 As the Father has loved me, so have I loved you, so continue in my love.

10 If you keep my commandments, you shall abide in my love, even as I have kept my Father's commandments, and have abided in his love.

11 These things have I taught to you, that my joy might remain in you, and that your joy might be full.

12 This is my commandment, That you love one another, as I have loved you.

13 There is no 'Greater' love a person can have than this. That they lay down their lives for another, as a friend in the Father in heaven.

14 You are my friends, if you do what ever I command you.

15 From now on, I don't consider you servants, for a servant doesn't know what his lord does, but I have called you friends, for all things that I have heard of my

Father I have made known unto you.

16 You have not chosen me, but I have chosen you and ordained you that you should go out and bring forth fruit unto heaven and that your fruit, remain, that whatever you ask of the Father in my name, he may give it to you.

17 These things I command you, that you love one another.

18 If the world hates you, you know that it hated me first, before it hated you.

19 If you were of the world and it's nature, those of this world would love you for they love only their own, but because you are not of the nature of this world for I have chosen you from out of it, therefore they hate you.

20 Remember all I have said and taught you, for you are not greater than I am, If they have persecuted me, they will also persecute you, but there are those as disciples who adhere to my teachings, and they will also adhere to yours.

21 When they persecute and even kill some of you, they will do it because you are my apostles who spread my name's sake, because they refuse to believe in the Father in heaven who sent me.

22 If I had chosen not to come and show them they can't hide all their unrighteous and unholy ways of living in sin,

23 They would not hate me, or my Father.

24 If I had not done amongst them the miracles and works which no other man has ever done, they would not have been exposed of being guilty of sin, but now they have seen their guilt and hypocrisy and hate me and the Father who sent me.

25 But it will come to pass to disgrace the words used by David who was guilty of breaking their own written laws, 'They hated me without a cause.'

26 But when the Comforter comes unto you whom I will send from the Father, the Spirit of Truth which is sent from the Father, will also come to testify of me, (*Note* in Index)

27 And you will also bear witness, because you have been with me from the very beginning.

146

*Note Verse 26

Amen John I, chosen to be the "Spirit of Truth" to the doctrines of Jesus on Nov. 19, 1975, "resurrected" after a fatal accident. For 32 years of preparation and instruction, the Lord instructs Amen John I, to write of his truths and all the deceivers misrepresentations to subjugate many to Roman rule, under their doctrines.

*Note by the author;

Before I start Chapter 30, it should be noted, that much of what was told to the apostles, has for the last 20 centuries been a mockery of what they endured, by many of Judeo-Christian faith, due to the wrong perception taken by many of them. What Jesus told the apostles, was for them ONLY, and not this world dominated mentality that much of what he told the apostles they would go through after his persecution, is what ALL disciples were to anticipate as an end of the world "scenar-io." First of all "end of the world" to the ancients of yesteryear was a GENERAL terminology given to DEATH. When each and every person, "dies," it is "your" end of the world for you no long exist in it. Of all that Jesus tells the apostles, he is not giving this great advice that one day he will return and "get even," what he says, in not so many words, is that every person will FACE the CONSEQUENCES of their decisions regarding their SOULS at DEATH or "the end of the world." As time has passed though, religion has given what Jesus says prior to his demise in the flesh a role of self-importance for many and many of Judeo faith the misperceptions EVERY-THING "requires" a "sacrifice" to wash away sin. It's why so many Neanderthal ideologies and beliefs are part of Judeo-Christian doctrines. Vanity creates the sick need to include oneself in ritualistic practices which permeate the psychoses of being so important to Amen in heaven, even murder is condoned by him, "if" for the PROPER " cause. " In Judeo-Christian belief, PROPER because the BLOOD of JESUS "cleans" the slate of SIN, so he DIED for US as the LAMB OF GOD? Even the terms used by these religious is Neanderthal in nature. To THINK the murder of a "man," on the same level as that of a sacrificial "lamb." Jesus was MURDERED upon the orders of the Jewish peoples of his day at the hands of Romans NOT their "descendants," AND the APOSTLES, except for one, were put to death at the hands of those who rejected their doctrine, given them by Christ, NOT for any particular RACIAL motive, religious or otherwise. BLOOD does not "CLEANSE" the BAD BEHAVIORS of " ANYONE. " That " cleansing " can only be done by a person willing to make the EFFORTS it takes and YEARS it takes to be an EXCEPTION-

148

AL PERSON on earth as Jesus and his Apostles WERE on earth.

Of all the MIRACLES Jesus performed or his Apostles performed, NONE included INSTANT CURES for one's BEHAVIORS. Much of what Jesus taught, and his Apostles taught, were that DISCIPLINE and proper ATTITUDES are the avenues for changing ones self into a better person. Far too many DELUDE themselves to "think" outside the REALITIES of faith and miss the whole point of Jesus' mission on earth. Sure, the attitudes and behaviors of the Jews in his day were an important part of that mission, but they were not the only ones he MINISTER "to." One of the most important parts of his ministry was that people NEEDED to take RESPONSIB-ILITY for themselves and how they BEHAVED towards each other so as to EARN their way into heaven. Amen in heaven, made heaven a realm of PEACE, and 90% of people who consider they will be part of his realm, aren't even going to make it pass the first gate. Why? Too much vanity in what they believe will get them there. Just as you would not build a football stadium in the middle cemetery, Amen does not want all this shouting and yelling at the top of ones lungs amongst the peaceful. In all I judge, I judge righteously, for I have been THERE, "and" I have also been to the place of the damned. It was all part of the preparations the Lord in heaven put me through to see TRUTH, and WHY he asked me to write about it. In "death," I was resurrected to be one in Jesus, just as he is in the Father. My "holy spirit" IS he who came unto mankind several times, one of which was amongst the Jewish peoples as told, but not as told in ways of FAITH. The doctrines of Jesus have nothing to do with the God of Wrath of the Jewish peoples, and is why I was resurrected to write them according to the HOLY SPIRIT of he who is known as Jesus Christ, according to the ideology of Amen in heaven who gave that faith to pre-dynastic peoples of Egypt in his sacred language of hieroglyphics, and not the hypocrisy of present day.

149

CHAPTER 30

1 These things I have told you, are, so you won't say that I didn't warn you about how you too, will suffer at the hands of men,

2 They will put you out of their synagogues, and yes, the time will come when they will kill you and think they have done their God a favor.

3 And these things they will do to you because they have not known the Father in heaven nor me.

4 I have told you these things so that when the time comes, you will remember that I warned you beforehand of what will happen to you. I am telling you now, because I didn't warn you these things would happen to you since I have been with you.

5 But now I am getting ready to go unto the Father who sent me, none of you have asked me, Where are you going?

6 But because I have told you these things now, sorrow has filled your hearts.

7 Nevertheless, I tell you the truth, that it is necessary for you to know that I must leave you, because if I do not leave, the Comforter will not come unto you, but if I leave, I will comfort each one of you by sending unto you the holy spirit from heaven.

8 And when the holy spirit comes upon you, it will reprove the world of sin, righteousness, and judgment.

9 Of sin, because they refuse to believe in me,

10 Of righteousness, because I go unto my Father, and you won't see me anymore,

11 Of judgment, because the prince of this world is judged.

12 I have many things to teach you yet, but I can't tell you right now, because you wouldn't be able to bear them,

13 Later, when the Spirit of truth comes upon you, it will guide you into all the truths, for he will not speak of himself, but whatever he hears, that will he tell you and he will show you things to come.

14 He will glorify me, for he will receive wisdom from me, and show it unto you.

15 For all things that the Father is, I am, so therefore I say unto you, the Father will take of the powers over the flesh I have and give them unto you.

16 A little while later, you won't see me anymore, but again after a little while, you will see me before I go unto the Father in heaven."

17 Then some of his apostles began to discuss these matters he had just told them amongst themselves of what this means, 'A little while, and you will not see me, again, a little while, and you will see me, because I go to the Father?'

18 Discussing it further, 'What are this things Jesus if telling us will happen in, 'A little while?, It's hard to understand what he's talking about."

19 Jesus, perceiving the apostles were confused about what he said and desired for him to explain, said, "Are you confused over what I stated about, 'A little while later, you won't see me anymore, but again after a little while, you will see me again?.'

20 Amen-Ra says to tell you, verily that you will cry and feel depressed, while the world will rejoice that you are full of sorrow, but your sorrow will be turned into joy.

21 When a woman who is pregnant reaches labor she feels sorrow because she knows her hour has come, but as soon as she has delivered her child, she doesn't remember all the pain anymore for she is full of joy for the child she has given birth to and brought into the world.

22 You will feel the same kind of sorrow, but do not despair, for I will see you again and your heart will rejoice, joy that nobody can take away from you.

23 In hat day you won't ask me for anything. Amen-Ra says to tell you, verily, whatever you ask of the Father in my name, he will give it you.

24 So far you haven't ask me for anything, but later, ask so you will receive, that your joy may be full.

25 These things have I told you in predictions of later events, but the time will come , when I won't have to predict for they will be things you can plainly see for yourselves, which will reveal the Father in heaven unto you.

26 In that day you will ask in my name, and I will be with the Father to ask on your

behalf and able to fulfill your needs.

27 For the Father loves you, because you have loved me and have believed that I was his Son sent unto you.

28 I came from the Father in heaven to be born into this world. Again, I leave the world and go to be with the Father."

29 His Apostles said, "Now, we understand you plainly since you aren't speaking in parables.

30 We are sure now that your wisdom is from Amen in heaven and know all things, that nobody needs to ask you to prove yourself to them and by this we believe that you have come to us from Amen."

31 Jesus asked them, "So you now believe.

32 Behold, the time is getting close, yea, upon us, that you will scatter, for every man will take refuge to his own and shall leave me alone, but yet, I am not alone, because the Father is with me.

33 These things I have told you, that in me you might have peace. In the world you shall have hard times, but be of good cheer, for I have overcome the world."

CHAPTER 31

1 After he finished speaking to the Apostles, Jesus lifted up his eyes to heaven and said, "Father, the hour has come. Glorify your Son that your Son may also glorify you,

2 As you have given me power over all flesh, that I should give eternal life to as many as you have given me.

3 And this is life eternal, that they might know you are the only true Lord, and I am Yeshua (Jesus,) whom you have sent.

4 I have glorified you on the earth and have finished the work which you gave me to do.

5 And now, Oh Father, glorify in me, thine own self with the glory which I had with you before this world existed.

6 I have made known your name unto the men which you gave me from amongst those of this world, yours they remain for you gave them to me, and they have kept your teachings.

7 They have known that everything you have given me whatever it has been, is from you,

8 For I have given to them the teachings which you gave me and they have received them. They know that I came out from you and have also believed that you sent me.

9 I pray for them, not the world, for they are the ones you have given me, and are yours.

10 All who believe in me are also yours, just as yours are mine, and I am glorified in them.

11 Now, I will not be in this world much longer, but these apostles will be in the world, so I come unto you, Holy Father, to protect them through thine own name, these whom you have given me, that they may be as one, as we are.

12 While I have been with them in the world, I kept them in your name. None of them is lost, but Judas Iscariot,

13 I come before you and these things I speak in this world that they might have my joy fulfilled in themselves.

14 I have given them your teachings, and the world has hated them, because they are not of this world, just as I am not of the world.

15 I pray that you don't take them out of this world as of yet, but that you protect and keep them from evil.

16 They are not of the evils of this world, just as I am not.

17 Sanctify them through your truth, for your words are truth.

18 As you have sent me into this world to teach it of the Kingdom of heaven and eternal life, so do I send them out into the world to teach others the same.

19 For their sakes I sanctify myself, that they might also be sanctified through the truth.

20 I don't pray just for these alone, but for all the disciples who have believed in me and will believe in me through all the apostles teach of me,

21 That all the apostles may be as one, as you Father, are in me, and I am in you, that they also, may be one in us, so that the world may believe that you are the one who sent me.

22 The glory which you gave me, I have given unto them, that they may be one, just as we are one,

23 With me in them, and you in me, that they may be made perfect in one cause, that the world may know that you sent me and for what purpose, and have loved them, just as you have loved me.

24 Father, I also ask that those you have given me, be with me where I am, that they may see my glory which you have given me, for you have loved me even before this world existed.

25 Oh righteous Father, the world has not known you except for me and these who have known that you sent me.

26 And I have declared unto them your name in heaven of Amen, and they will declare it, that the love with which you have loved me may be in them, as I will be in them.

CHAPTER 32

1 When Jesus was done talking, he and the apostles went over the brook Cedron, a place called Gethsemane where there was a garden, which all of them entered. Jesus told his apostles, "Sit here, while I go over there by myself to pray."

2 Judas who was about to betray him, also knew the place where many times Jesus and the apostles would come together to be with each other.

3 Before Jesus went to pray, he took Peter aside and told him that he needed alittle time to himself to pray since the hour of his apprehension was drawing near.

4 The rest of the Apostles were deeply concerned, but Jesus said, "I am just feeling the sorrow of the moment, stay here and watch that no one interrupts me while I pray."

5 As Jesus went in secret he prayed unto the Father in heaven the prayer he taught unto his apostles to give him strength.

6 After, Jesus returned to find the apostles all asleep and woke Peter up and said, "Peter, wake up, even in my last hours none of you could stay awake to watch out for when they come for me?

7 Watch and pray to give you strength so that none of you fall to temptation, for indeed the spirit is willing, but the flesh is weak."

8 Jesus went away alone to pray in secret a second time,

9 When he returned, again he found the apostles asleep, as they were very tired.

10 So Jesus went away again to pray for a third time.

11 When he returned unto the apostles he thought to himself, "You can sleep now for it doesn't matter now that the hour has come,.." just then one of the apostles awoke and said,

12 "Wake up!, Jesus is back," but just as they were getting up to their feet,

13 The Jewish chief priests and elders showed up with soldiers and Judas, one of the twelve chosen by Jesus who betrayed him, along with many other that had swords and staffs with them.

14 Judas Iscariot, beforehand, advised the priest and elders that upon coming to

Jesus and the apostles he would give them a sign letting them know who was his Master Jesus was. A kiss to his cheek.

15 As they all stood there, Judas walked up to Jesus and kissed him on the cheek.

16 Jesus said unto him, "Friend, your sin is forgiven," then they arrested Jesus and began to take him away.

17 Immediately one of the apostles drew out a sword and struck one of the servants of the high priest with it and cut off an ear.

18 Jesus said unto him, "Put that sword away, don't you know that those who live by the sword will accomplish nothing except to die by it. Have I not taught you the ways of peace?

19 Don't you think that if I were of the nature of the devil, I couldn't summon legions of angels to defend me?

20 But I am of the Lord of love, not hate, and of the nature only the Father in heaven understands, which one day, hopefully mankind will know."

21 Jesus then turned to the peoples who came to arrest him and said, "Am I such a criminal that you need to come unto me with swords and staffs? It is I, whom you sat down daily with, teaching you in the temple, and you never laid a hand on me," and even then Jesus saw his apostles desert him.

22 But this happened just as Jesus had told them, and which they denied. In the last hour, none had the courage to stand up for him, but fled instead.

23 Jesus was lead down the streets of Jerusalem in the night like a common thief by his adversaries, to be taken before the high priest Caiaphas and the rest of the priests, scribes and elders who convened to condemn him.

24 Peter followed them from afar until they got to the high priest's palace and all of them went in, including Peter who sat with the servants to see the inquiry.

25 As the chief priests, and elders convened the council, they began the proceedings by bringing in many false witnesses against Jesus seeking to coherse a decision of putting him to death,

26 But each false charge failed, as they couldn't find one of them that bore enough evidence against him, though many false witnesses came. Then two more wit-

nesses came forward to testify against Jesus,

27 And said, "This fellow said, I am able to destroy the temple of the Lord, and can rebuild it in three days."

28 Caiaphas got up from his seat and said to Jesus, "What say you? Nothing? Did you say these blasphemous words these witnesses are accusing you of?"

29 But Jesus said nothing, and kept quiet. Then Caiaphas questioned him further, asking, "I order you by the living God, that you tell us whether you are this divine man prophesied about and said to be the Son of the Lord."

30 Jesus answered him, "You say so, nevertheless I say to you, after this day, you will see the Son of the 'true' living Father in heaven, who is Amen, and I will sit at his right hand of power and return upon the clouds of heaven."

31 Then Caiaphas fiercely tore his priestly garment apart at the collar and held his head in his hands as he dropped to his knees and yelled at the top of his lungs at Jesus saying, "By his own mouth this man defies our God with his blasphemies what further need do we have of witnesses? All of you can attest to it by what he just said.

32 What is the council's decision?" They furiously answered, "Guilty! Guilty and should be put to death!"

33 Then the priests and elders who condemned him came up to him and spit in his face, and repeatedly slapped and hit him with the palms of their hands,

34 Mocking and sarcastically saying, "Prophesy to us, Son of this God Amen, tell us, what's the name of the one who is hitting you?"

35 As all this was taking place, Peter couldn't take seeing this happen to Jesus anymore, so he went and sat outside the palace when a young woman was walking by , came up to him and said, "You're one of the ones who was with Jesus of Galilee."

36 Peter quickly replied, "I don't know who this Jesus you speak of happens to be," before everyone outside the palace.

CHAPTER 33

1 Right away, Peter went home and sat out on his porch, when another woman saw him and said to those sitting on the porch with Peter, "This man was also with Jesus of Nazareth.

2 Again, Peter denied swearing an oath that he didn't know who Jesus was.

3 After a while, some of the people who were at the palace saw him as they were walking by began to point in the direction of Peter and said, "Look, there's that man who was at the palace, he surely is one of those who is a disciple of that man Jesus, for he talks just like him."

4 Peter got angry and began to curse and swear at the people who were pointing at him and said,"I told you at the palace, I didn't know this man Jesus now get off my property." As he did, immediately a rooster began to crow.

5 It was then that Peter remembered what Jesus had told him would happen and how he would deny him three times before dawn. He began to cry bitterly and left.

6 As morning came, all the Jewish chief priests and elders of the peoples went into a chamber to discuss how they would put Jesus to death,

7 They decided to take him before the Roman governor, Pontius Pilate, so that they could say the Romans had him executed so they put Jesus in shackles and took him before Pilate.

8 Judas Iscariot, at about the same time, felt remorse over having betrayed Jesus, seeing the ways he was condemned and mistreated, and repented. He immediately went to return the thirty pieces of silver to the chief priests and elders, thinking that maybe they would take the money back and release Jesus,

9 When he went in to see Caiaphas, the chief priests and elders, he said, "I have sinned in that I have betrayed innocent blood." They said, "What is that to us? You got what we agreed upon."

10 In despair, he threw the thirty pieces of silver on the floor of the temple, and left. Judas was so depressed over what he had done he went and hung himself.

11 After Judas left the temple, the chief priests picked up the pieces of silver, and

Caiaphas said, "It isn't lawful to put the money back in the treasury, as it was the price paid for blood."

12 After discussing it for awhile, they decided to buy a piece of land and use it as a potter's field to bury strangers in.

13 Whereupon that field was called, 'The field of blood,' unto this day.

14 This happened as one of the Hebrew prophets, Jeremiah predicted would happen in his prophesy, stating, "And they took the thirty pieces of silver, the price of him that was valued, whom they of the children of Israel did value,

15 And gave them for the potter's field, as the Lord appointed me."

16 As Jesus stood before the Roman governor, Pilate asked him, "Are you the King of the Jews? Jesus answered, "So you say."

17 When Jesus was accused by the chief priests and elders, in front of Pilate, he answered nothing.

18 Then Pilate said to Jesus, "Don't you hear all the things they are accusing you of?" But Jesus just looked at Pilate, and did not utter a word, which amazed the Roman governor, for he'd never seen a man who did not plead for his life who faced death. At that he greatly admired his courage.

20 At this time, was a feast taking place for the Roman governor and it was customary for authorities to release a prisoner from prison whom the peoples wanted released.

21 In prison, was a notable prisoner, called Barabbas, guilty of murder, whom the peoples wanted brought out.

22 When the soldiers brought out Barabbas, they put him and Jesus side by side upon a platform for everyone who was gathered there to see. Pilate said to them, "Who do you want me to release to you? Barabbas, a murderer or Jes us who calls himself the Son of the Lord."

23 Pilate knew that the Jewish priests were envious of this man Jesus and what they were up to. For awhile the peoples talked amongst themselves.

24 So Pilate sat down upon his seat and as he did, his wife came up to him and said, "Have nothing to do with the persecution of this just man, because I suffered the

loss of alot of sleep last night having one nightmare after another because of this man.

25 Out in the crowd, the chief priests and elders persuaded the peoples that they should ask for Barabbas, and have Jesus put to death.

26 When the governor asked, "So which of the two am I to release to you?" As if together they shouted out, "Barabbas. Give us Barrabbas."

27 Pilate asked them, "And what am I to do with this man Jesus, who calls himself a Son of Amen in heaven?" And the crowd shouted back, "Crucify him."

28 Then Pilate asked, "Why?, what evil has this man done? Why not Barabbas, who deserves to die?" But the crowd yelled even louder, "Crucify Jesus!"

29 When Pilate saw that he accomplished nothing but to stir up the crowd, he wanted no part of it and took some water and washed his hands before the multitude of Jewish peoples, saying, "It is your decision. I am innocent of killing this just person, and so it will be done as you ask."

30 Then the peoples answered him, "His blood be on us, and on our children."

31 Then Pilate released Barabbas unto them, and told the soldiers to take him and prepare him to be crucified.

32 Then the soldiers of the governor took Jesus into the common hall, and gathered many soldiers around him.

33 They stripped him, and hung him against the wall and gave him many lashes with a leather whip, then took him down and put a scarlet robe on him,

34 Laughing, one of the soldiers went and gathered branches of thorns which he wove into a crown and forced it upon the head of Jesus, another soldier put a reed in his right hand, while they all laughingly got on their knees before him in mockery, stating, "All hail to the King of the Jews!"

CHAPTER 34

1 Then all the soldiers spit on Jesus, took the reed out of his hand while one of them hit him on the head knocking him to the floor,

2 After mocking Jesus, the soldiers lifted him up, took the scarlet robe off him, put his own raiment on his shoulders and led him away to be crucified.

3 As they came out, the soldiers grabbed a man from amongst the crowd, a man called Simon from Cyrene and made him carry the wooden cross, Jesus was to be hung upon.

4 Jesus was partly disoriented and bleeding, but even then, he was made to bear the weight of the cross part of the way until they reached the place called Golgotha, referred to as a place of a skull,

5 Jesus was given vinegar to drink mingled with gall, but when he tasted it, he wouldn't drink.

6 After he was laid on the cross by the roman soldiers and nails driven through his wrists and feet, while some of them took his garments and began to gamble for them,

7 Many sat down on the ground as the soldiers lifted him up on the cross into the middle hole that had been dug to plant the cross in.

8 Above the head of Jesus, in mockery, the soldiers placed the inscription on the cross, "KING OF THE JEWS."

9 Two thieves were also crucified along with Jesus, one on the right hand, and the other, on the left.

10 As soon as the soldiers were done with all three being crucified, people began to line up to make fun of Jesus, while many wagged their heads in Jewish ritualistic contempt exclaiming,

11 "Hey You, who proclaims you can destroy the temple and rebuild it in three days. Save yourself. You say you're the Son of Amen, let us see your powers and come down from the cross."

12 In the same manner the chief priests, scribes and elders mocked him, and said,

13 "This man is said to have saved so many others he can't even save himself. If he's this 'King' so many proclaim him to be, then he will come down from the cross, and 'then' we'll believe him.

14 He trusted in Amen, let him deliver him now, if he will have him, for he said, 'I am the Son of Amen.'"

15 The thieves which were crucified with him, also cast doubt at him.

16 Now from the sixth hour there was darkness over all the land until the ninth hour.

17 At about the ninth hour Jesus cried out in a loud voice, "Elio, Elio, lama sabachthani?," translated from Aramaic means, 'My Lord, my Lord, why have you forsaken me?'

18 The persons who were standing near him, heard what he said and said, "This man is calling out to Elijah."

19 Immediately one of them ran, got a sponge and dipped it in vinegar putting it on a pole to give Jesus a drink.

20 The rest of those there said, "Forget that, let's see if Elijah shows up to save him."

21 But at that moment Jesus cried out again, in a loud voice, and died.

22 As he did, across Jerusalem the veil of the temple tore from the top to the bottom, the earth shook, and huge rocks broke apart,

23 Alot of graves opened up, as the bodies of the saints which slept arose,

24 As happened also after the resurrection of Jesus later, and these people who came out of their graves, went into the holy city and appeared to many.

25 Now when the centurion and the others who were there when Jesus died, watching, saw the earthquake and those things that happened and very afraid, and the centurion said, "Truly this was the Son of the Lord."

26 Alot of women were there, standing afar, who had followed Jesus from Galilee, ministered to the centurion,

27 Among them, Mary Magdalene, Mary, the mother of Jesus, James and Joses, and the mother of Zebedee's children.

28 In the evening, a rich man of Arimathea named Joseph, himself a disciple of Jesus,

29 Went to Pilate, and begged for the body of Jesus. Pilate agreed and commanded the body to be delivered to Joseph.

30 The body of Jesus was delivered to Joseph, and he wrapped it in clean linen, as everyone was there with Joseph waiting for it to be delivered.

31 Joseph laid the body in a new tomb he had reserved for himself, he made having cut it out rock on his property. Once the body of Jesus was inside, they prayed and the women and some of Jesus disciples spent awhile with the body, one of which was Mary his mother. After, Joseph and some of the disciples rolled a huge heavy stone in place over the entrance to the sepulcher, and some of them left, including Joseph.

32 Outside the sepulcher, Mary Magdalene, the mother of Jesus, Mary, and many of the disciples of Jesus sat grieving over his death.

CHAPTER 35

1 The next day that followed, the chief priests and Pharisees came together up to the governor's palace to talk to Pilate,

2 When they were taken before the governor they said, "Sir, we remember that the deceiver said while he was alive, 'After three days I will rise again.'

3 Command therefore that the sepulcher be made secure until the third day, that his disciples won't come by night and steal the body so as to proclaim falsely unto the peoples that he has risen from the dead, thus making the situation of this man and his false doctrines even worse."

4 Then Pilate said, "That's you're responsibility if you're so afraid of being made to look like fools. Go away and leave me out of your matters and secure the sepulcher yourselves."

5 So they went and made the sepulcher secure, sealing the stone, and setting a watch day and night to make sure nobody stole the body.

6 At the end of the sabbath as it began to dawn toward the first day of the week, came Mary Magdalene and the Mary, Jesus' mother to see the sepulcher.

7 There was a great earthquake felt throughout Jerusalem as an angel of the Lord descended from heaven upon the sepulcher. Once there the angel rolled the stone from the entrance door, and sat upon it.

8 His appearance was as that of lightning, and his clothes, white as snow,

9 The guards which the chief priests and Pharisees had placed to secure the sepulcher, were in such terror they literally turned pale as dead men and nervously shook at the sight of the angel. As fast as they realized what had happened, they ran away as fast as they could.

10 The angel saw the two women approaching the sepulcher and said, "Don't be afraid, for I know you seek Jesus who was crucified.

11 He is not here, for he has risen, as he said he would after three days. Come, see for yourselves where the Lord lay, and that he is amongst the living.

12 Go quickly and tell his disciples that he is risen from the dead, and to hurry, for

he will appear to them in Galilee just as he told them. There you will see him."

13 And both women departed quickly from the sepulcher, scared but overjoyed, ran as fast as they could to tell the Apostles.

14 As they were running to tell the Apostles, Jesus met them, saying, " Hello. " Immediately they recognized who it was and dropped to his feet and were so happy to see him.

15 Then Jesus said to them, "Don't be afraid, go tell my Apostles to go to Galilee, and there, they can see me."

16 The two women went and delivered Jesus' message to the Apostles. At about the same time, the guards who ran from the sepulcher came before the chief priests and told them an angel had appeared and rolled the stone and there was no body in the sepulcher. After going to check for themselves,

17 They assembled a council of all the priests and elders together. There they came to a decision to give a large sum of money to the guards and as many soldiers as they could to spread the rumor,

18 Saying, "His disciples came by night, and stole his body while all of us slept.

19 And if the governor happens to hear this rumor, we'll tell him we heard it too so you won't get in trouble."

20 So they took the money, and did as they were told and this rumor is commonly believed amongst the Jews to this day.

21 The eleven disciples who left to go to Galilee, went up into a mountain where Jesus had told them before he would appear.

22 There, he appeared unto them, while some of them worshiped him, and others doubted.

23 Jesus spoke to them and said, "All power is given to me in heaven and on earth.

24 Go out therefore and teach all nations, baptizing them in the name of the Father, Son, and Holy Spirit,

25 Teaching them to observe all things whatsoever I have commanded you, and re-member, I am with you always, even unto the end of the world. Amen."

CONCLUSION

In conclusion, of all that presently is written and passed off as being the "books" and "truth" about Jesus, not one scholar in all the centuries of existence has examin-" basic " truths. COMMON SENSE and LOGIC. Jesus and his Apostles spoke " Aramaic, " so should not their " writings " have also been done in their chosen language? What the world has been lead to believe are the original manuscripts in Hebrew and Greek are nothing more than "Romanized," and NOT truthful. One "basic" fact which brings about this conclusion is in what Jerome, who wrote the Latin Vulgate, put within his "translation." The name of Lord in heaven, not as Yahveh or Jehovah, but "Amen," just as it was written in the Aramaic gospels. What the world has been lead to believe were "books" written by the apostles, including the Apostle Paul's letters in Greek and Hebrew are the works of the "DECIEVERS," and is why you find many things in them to connect Jesus and those apostles to a Jewish lineage. To do a THOROUGH acceptance of TRUTH, anyone with "common sense" and "logic" in an attribute towards faith, should always leave out of that truth, EMOTIION and FANATICISM, to obtain basic CELESTIAL KNOWLEDGE. I have always been surprised to find, that so many "Doctors," OR "experts," of theology, as they want to "consider" themselves, have not taken a good look at one FACT which an extremely "basic" one. LANGUAGE. I have seen many scholars, maniacally dissecting the Greek and Hebrew manuscripts, "SUPPOSEDLY," the REAL works of the APOSTLES, DISCIPLES, and LETTERS of PAUL (Saul), BUT they never "ask" themselves the most obvious oddity which is so transparent about all that is written and said to be the truths of Jesus from his Apostles and Disciples. The LANGUAGES they are all written in. The reason I have always chosen to believe more in what Matthew wrote above that any other Apostle, is his level of "education." You had to have one to be employed to collect taxes, at least have a working knowledge of mathematics. Psychologically an "analytical" MIND. The one thing not many ponder in all that is written about Jesus by his Apostles and disciples is their level of education. Works said to have been written by John, James, Peter, and some of the other Apostles come into question when you ask yourself, where did they obtain an educatio when most of the Jewish population at the time was illiterate. Not that fishermen were "dummer," but Matthew was a public official, and as such, obviously, EDUCATED. Unlike Paul, Matthew was WITH Jesus, and unlike the works of everyone else, his works were not in the language of Aramaic, Hebrew or Greek. His book was written in Syro-Chaldaic. The "only" one in the language which came from the upper northern parts of Israel. It is the TRANSLATIONS and MEN of "deception" which have lead the world to believe in many falsehoods and lies about WHO Jesus and the apostles WERE, and in all that transpired over 2000 years ago. There is one other CONNECTION which scholars have never looked at in REFORMATIONS of faith. IMPERIALISTIC influences, or that of leaderships of EMPIRES. AT about the fall of the Egyptian Empire, any scholar can find JUDA-ISM'S start. At the fall of Grecian Empire, by the conquering by the Roman Empire, you will find the creation of CHRISTIANITY. Again, a little over 500 years later, you will find the fall of the Roman Empire, "and" the creation of the religion of ISLAM. Coincidence? I don't think so. " Conquerors " ALSO conquer weak "MEN-TALITIES" and in ancient times these conquerors WERE the CREATORS of the RELIGIONS they used to SUBJUDGATE their subjects. It IS why you have this great DECEPTION of all that was once TRUE. To every CONQUEROR, and to every IGNORANT person they feed their propaganda and put under their thumb in the faiths they forced on peoples according to THEIR "doctrines," is a faithful servant of the Empire, in taxes, WAR and anything these conquerers willed through their God (s). One of the biggest reasons that every region has it's own religions and will KILL to defend those beliefs, IS, that these conquerors have been very wise not to allow the masses under them to gain a working knowledge of the world through literacy. It is why you hear within many of these religions that their "holy words" were passed down generation upon generation by "mouth" because not many of them knew how to READ or WRITE. One truth did come out of all that was given to humanity by the Lord though, and that is that with all their efforts of Empires to deceive using the original works given, the rewritten words they fed the masses left enough truth in them to discern "it," find out who the Father in heaven really "is," and all he willed for us to learn from him, which by the way was not this God of Wrath, who happens to be the "devil." The ULTIMATE FACT which I present to all those who read all I have ever written about that FATHER in heaven is in who I AM as his Spirit of Truth to bring the message Jesus wanted and told of, in that he was Yeshua, the THEBAN "divine child" and Son of the living Lord in heaven sent down to teach of HIS nature, no religion, has discerned even to this day. It is also the reason Jewish leaders had him EXECUTED in 26 a.d. A "culture" bent on deceiving the world that everything sacred is EVIL, when "history" itself shows the world the truth, including that of their EXODUS and SLAVERY to Egypt. The ancient Israelites, WERE the descendants of the Hyksos, who were RUTHLESS peoples, just like the Persians and Romans. As conquerors, they were not satisfied with just defeating an enemy, but would resort to slaughtering EVERYONE, including women and children of their enemies.

The message of Jesus was pure and "simple" no matter what you misperceive a God to be. This SPECIES "is" of the world and "it's" GOD. To CHANGE who we ARE in the FLESH is IMPOSSIBLE, and he used his Apostles to prove that point, for even the BEST in faith, in the flesh, will fail. Jesus, just as Amen in heaven DO "exist," just as Jesus exists in me, he can exist in you, and if he exists in you so does his FATHER. Humanity, no matter how hard it TRYS will NEVER achieve the kind of nature they possess here on earth, for it is an impossibility within the nature of a place ruled by it's God, the Devil, and all the unpredictable catastrophes either by nature or mankind. All mankind can do, is to UNITE against the odds and help each other through the worse of times in the HOPES some of the children do not suffer to grow up into tyrants that inflict injury and death upon the rest of the human race. As long as the past "agonies" of mankind remain active in the minds of the vengeful, no peace will ever exist either. DECISIONS which are unpopular, sooner or later will HAVE TO be made by this species if it is to survive extinction. "Ridding" itself of it's own bad elements, instead of making excuses for them and tolerating them. That means "executing" those who are incorrigible. Like it or "not." Make extreme

168

LAWS that stiffen the penalties to those who think they can get away with subjecting mankind to their bad behaviors. QUIT housing them while punishing the innocent to a lifetime of supporting the worthless in prisons who choose to never change for it only DRAINS resources from all the ones who work hard to be productive members of society. These are not solutions of "heaven," but solutions of the "earth" and the FLESH. To SOLVE that which presents ever cycling problems, "demands" not spiritual solutions, but solutions which will always be unpopular to everyone and religions, but history teaches us that many of the religious have not been the best examples themselves. Religions complain of the lack of help of governments to feed the hungry, but with their own resources, put up ridiculous buildings. They complain against those who choose not to care for children, but will not house any of the unwanted themselves. They talk of "immorality," but take the side of bad priests and ministers.. Hypocrites? Jesus said it best. The "PERFECT" faith is that of LOVING ONE ANOTHER like each person loves themselves. When that happens, you will Love in the one and only Lord, ...**AMEN IN HEAVEN**, and **"his"** real teachings and **FAITH.**

Iesu Christi dico qua Amen dico,

"Mandatum novum do vobis ut diligatis invlcem sicut dilexi vos ut et vos diligatis invicem in hoc cognoscent omnes quia mei discipuli estis si dilectionem habueritis ad invicem"

(Jerome - Latin Vulgate, 4th century a.d.)

Translated - Jesus Christ says that Amen says,

"A new commandment I give unto you, That ye love one another, as I have loved you, that ye also love one another. By this shall all men know that ye are my disciples, if ye have love one to another.

(King James Version – 1611 a.d.)

Made in the USA
Monee, IL
31 October 2019